DAYS WITHOUT END

Eugene O'Neill

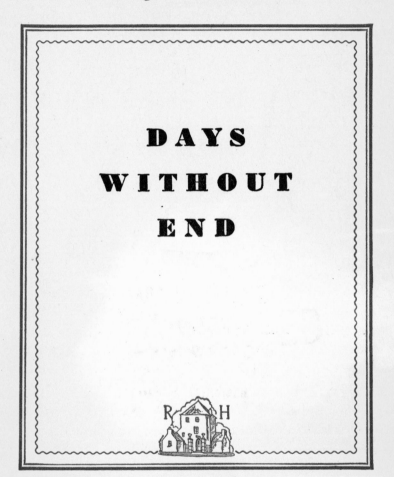

DAYS
WITHOUT
END

RANDOM HOUSE
NEW YORK

COPYRIGHT, 1934, BY EUGENE O'NEILL

812

O'N

First Edition
Published, January, 1934

PRINTED IN THE UNITED STATES OF AMERICA
BY VAN REES PRESS, NEW YORK CITY

To
CARLOTTA

DAYS WITHOUT END

CHARACTERS

(In the order in which they appear)

JOHN

LOVING

WILLIAM ELIOT

FATHER MATTHEW BAIRD

ELSA, *John Loving's wife*

MARGARET

LUCY HILLMAN

DR. HERBERT STILLWELL

NURSE

SCENES

Act One

PLOT FOR A NOVEL

Scene—John Loving's office in the offices of Eliot and Company, New York City—an afternoon in early Spring, 1932.

Act Two

PLOT FOR A NOVEL (CONTINUED)

Scene—Living-room of the Lovings' duplex apartment—later the same afternoon.

Act Three

PLOT FOR A NOVEL (CONTINUED)

Scene One—The living-room again—evening of the same day.
Scene Two—John Loving's study—later that night.

Act Four

THE END OF THE END

Scene One—The study and Elsa's bedroom—a little before dawn of a day about a week later.
Scene Two—The interior of a church—a few minutes later.

ACT ONE

PLOT FOR A NOVEL

DAYS WITHOUT END

ACT ONE

SCENE—JOHN LOVING's *private office in the offices of* ELIOT AND COMPANY, *New York City. On the left, a window. Before it, a chair, its back to the window, and a table. At rear of table, an armchair, facing front. A third chair is at right of table. In the rear wall, a door leading to the outer offices. At center of the room, toward right, another chair.*

It is afternoon of a cloudy day in Spring, 1932. The light from the window is chill and gray. At the rise of the curtain, this light is concentrated around the two figures seated at the table. As the action goes on, the light imperceptibly spreads until, at the close of the opening scene between JOHN *and* LOVING, *it has penetrated to all parts of the room.*

JOHN *is seated in the chair at left of desk. He is forty, of medium height. His face is handsome, with the rather heavy, conventional American type of good looks—a straight nose and a square jaw, a wide mouth that has an incongruous feminine sensitiveness, a broad forehead, blue eyes. He is dressed in a dark suit, white shirt and collar, a dark tie, black shoes and socks.*

LOVING *sits in the armchair at rear of table. He is the same age, of the same height and figure, is dressed in every detail exactly the same. His hair is the same—dark, streaked with gray. In contrast to this similarity between the two, there is an equally strange dissimilarity. For* LOVING's *face is a mask whose features reproduce exactly the features of* JOHN's *face—the death mask of a* JOHN *who has died with a sneer of scornful mockery on his lips. And this mocking scorn is repeated in the expression of the eyes which stare bleakly from behind the mask.*

JOHN *nervously writes a few words on a pad—then stops abruptly and stares before him.* LOVING *watches him.*

LOVING
(His voice singularly toneless and cold but at the same time insistent)

Surely, you don't need to make any more notes for the second part—your hero's manhood up to the time he *(A sneer comes into his voice)* at last finds love. I should think you could remember that—only too well.

JOHN
(Mechanically)

Yes.

LOVING
(Sneeringly)

As for the third part, I know you have the most vivid recollection of his terrible sin.

16

JOHN

Don't mock, damn you!

LOVING

So it's only in the last part that you will have to use your imagination. How are you going to end this interesting plot of yours? Given your hero's ridiculous conscience, what happens then?

JOHN

He has the courage to confess—and she forgives.

LOVING

The wish is father to that thought, eh? A pretty, sentimental ending—but a bit too pointed, don't you think? I'm afraid she might begin to wonder—

JOHN

(*Apprehensively*)

Yes. That's true.

LOVING

I advise you to make the last part so obviously fictitious that it will kill any suspicion which might be aroused by what has gone before.

JOHN

How can I end it, then?

LOVING

(*After a second's pause—in a voice he tries to make casual but which is indefinably sinister*)

Why not have the wife die?

JOHN

(*Starts—with a shudder*)

Damn you! What makes you think of that?

LOVING

Why, nothing—except I thought you'd agreed that the further removed from present actuality you make your ending, the better it will be.

JOHN

Yes—but—

LOVING

(*Mockingly*)

I hope you don't suspect some hidden, sinister purpose behind my suggestion.

JOHN

I don't know. I feel— (*Then as if desperately trying to shake off his thoughts*) No! I won't think of it!

LOVING

And I was thinking, too, that it would be interesting to work out your hero's answer to his problem, if his wife died, and imagine what he would do with his life then.

JOHN

No! Damn you, stop making me think—!

LOVING

Afraid to face your ghosts—even by proxy? Surely, even you can have that much courage!

18

JOHN

It is dangerous—to call things.

LOVING

Still superstitious? Well, I hope you realize I'm only trying to encourage you to make something of this plot of yours more significant—for your soul, shall I say?—than a cowardly trick!

JOHN

You know it's more than that. You know I'm doing it to try and explain to myself, as well as to her.

LOVING

(*Sneeringly*)

To excuse yourself to yourself, you mean! To lie and escape admitting the obvious natural reason for—

JOHN

You lie! I want to get at the real truth and understand what was behind—what evil spirit of hate possessed me to make me—

LOVING

(*Contemptuously—but as he goes on a strange defiant note of exultance comes into his voice*)

So it's come back to that again, eh? Your old familiar nightmare! You poor, damned superstitious fool! I tell you again what I have always told you: There is nothing—nothing to hope for, nothing to fear—neither devils nor gods—nothing at all!

DAYS WITHOUT END

(*There is a knock on the door at rear.* JOHN *immediately pretends to be writing. At the same time his features automatically assume the meaninglessly affable expression which is the American business man's welcoming poker face.* LOVING *sits motionlessly regarding him with scornful eyes.*)

JOHN

(*Without looking up, calls*)

Come in. (*The door in rear is half opened and* WILLIAM ELIOT, JOHN LOVING'S *partner, looks in. He is about forty, stout, with a prematurely bald head, a round face, a humorous, good-natured mouth, small eyes behind horn-rimmed spectacles.*)

ELIOT

Hello, John. Busy?

JOHN

Foolish question, Bill.

ELIOT

(*His eyes pass over* LOVING *without seeing him. He does not see him now or later. He sees and hears only* JOHN, *even when* LOVING *speaks. And it will be so with all the characters. They are quite unaware of* LOVING'S *existence, although at times one or another may subtly sense his presence.* ELIOT *comes forward. He says jokingly*)

You sound downhearted, John. Don't let our little depression get you. There's always the poorhouse. Quite cozy, too, they say. Peace for the weary—

20

LOVING

(*Cuts in—mockingly*)

There is much to be said for peace.

ELIOT

(*As if it were* JOHN *who had spoken*)

Yes, John, there sure is—these damned days. (*Then giving* JOHN *a glance of concern*) Look here. I think our troubles are getting your nerve. You've seemed worn ragged lately. Why not take a few days in the country?

JOHN

Nonsense! I'm fine. (*Forcing a humorous tone*) What, besides the poorhouse, is on your mind, Bill?

ELIOT

Nothing but lunch. Ate too much again, damn it. What were you doping out when I came in? Got some new scheme for us?

JOHN

No.

LOVING

Merely trying to work out the answer to a puzzle—a human puzzle.

JOHN

(*Hurriedly*)

That is, I'm playing around with a plot for a novel that's come into my mind lately.

ELIOT

(*With amused surprise*)

What? Good God, don't tell me the literary bug is biting you again? I thought you'd got that out of your system long ago when you got engaged to Elsa and decided to come in with me and make some money.

JOHN

Well, I thought I might as well do something with all this leisure. Oh, I'll probably never write it, but it's amusing to dope out.

ELIOT

Why shouldn't you write it? You certainly showed you could write in the old days—articles, anyway. (*Then with a grin*) Why, I can remember when I couldn't pick up an advanced-thinker organ without running into a red-hot article of yours denouncing Capitalism or religion or something.

JOHN

(*Smiling good-naturedly*)

You always did have a mean memory, Bill.

ELIOT

(*Laughs*)

God, John, how you've changed! What hymns of hate you used to emit against poor old Christianity! Why, I remember one article where you actually tried to prove that no such figure as Christ had ever existed.

LOVING

(*His tone suddenly cold and hostile*)

I still feel the same on that subject.

ELIOT

(*Gives* JOHN *a surprised glance*)

Feel? Can't understand any one having feelings any more on such a dead issue as religion.

JOHN

(*Confused*)

Well, to tell the truth, I haven't given it a thought in years, but— (*Then hurriedly*) But, for Pete's sake, let's not get started on religion.

ELIOT

(*Changes the subject tactfully*)

Tell me about this novel of yours, John. What's it all about?

JOHN

Nothing to tell yet. I haven't got it finally worked out.

LOVING

The most important part, that is—the end.

JOHN

(*In a joking tone*)

But when I have, Bill, I'll be only too glad to get your esteemed criticism.

ELIOT

That's a promise, remember— (*Then getting up*) Well, I suppose I better get back to my office. (*He starts for the door*

23

—then turns back) Oh, I knew there was something I'd forgotten to tell you. Lucy Hillman called up while you were out.

JOHN

(*Carelessly*)

Yes? What did she want?

ELIOT

Wanted you. Got my office by mistake. She'll call up later. It was important, she said to tell you.

JOHN

Her idea of important! Probably wants my advice on what to give Walter for a birthday present.

ELIOT

What the devil's got into Walter lately, anyway? Getting drunk as a pastime may have its points, but as an exclusive occupation— Not to mention all his affairs with women. How does Lucy stand it? But I hear she's going to pieces, too.

JOHN

I don't believe it. She isn't the kind to have affairs.

ELIOT

I don't mean that. I mean booze.

JOHN

Oh. Well, if it's true, you can hardly blame her.

ELIOT

There are children, aren't there? Why hasn't she the guts to divorce him?

24

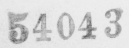

JOHN

Don't ask me. We haven't seen much of Lucy, either, for a long time. (*He dismisses the subject by looking down at his pad, as if he wanted to start writing.*)

ELIOT

(*Taking the hint*)

Well, I'll move along.

JOHN

See you later, Bill. (ELIOT *goes out, rear. After the door closes behind him* JOHN *speaks tensely*) Why did she phone? Important, she said. What can have happened?

LOVING

(*Coldly*)

Who knows? But you know very well she can't be trusted. You'd better be prepared for any stupid folly. And better get the end of your novel decided upon, so you can tell your plot —before it's too late.

JOHN

(*Tensely*)

Yes.

LOVING

(*the hidden sinister note again creeping into his coldly casual tone*)

There can be only one sensible, logical end for your hero, after he has lost his wife forever—that is, provided he loves her as much as he boasts to himself he does—and if he has any honor or courage left!

25

JOHN

(*Gives a start—then bitterly*)

Ah! I see now what you're driving at! And you talk of courage and honor! (*Defiantly*) No! He must go on! He must find a faith—somewhere!

LOVING

(*An undercurrent of anger in his sneering*)

Somewhere, eh? Now I wonder what hides behind that somewhere? Is it your old secret weakness—the cowardly yearning to go back—?

JOHN

(*Defensively*)

I don't know what you're thinking about.

LOVING

You lie! I know you! And I'll make you face it in the end of your story—face it and kill it, finally and forever! (*There is again a knock on the door and* JOHN's *eyes go to his pad. This time* ELIOT *comes in immediately, without waiting for an answer.*)

JOHN

Hello, Bill. What's up now?

ELIOT

(*Comes forward, a twinkle in his eye*)

John, there's a mysterious visitor outside demanding to see you.

26

JOHN

You mean—Lucy?

ELIOT

Lucy? No. This is a man. He ran into me before he got to Miss Sims and asked for you. (*Grinning*) And as it's liable to be a bitter blow, I thought I better break the news in person.

JOHN

What's the joke? Who is it?

ELIOT

It's a priest.

JOHN

A priest?

LOVING

(*Harshly*)

I don't know any priests! Tell him to get out!

ELIOT

Now don't be disrespectful. He claims he's your uncle.

JOHN

My uncle? Did he give his name?

ELIOT

Yes. Father Baird. Said he'd just got in from the West.

JOHN

(*Dumbfounded—forcing a smile*)

Well, I'll be damned.

27

ELIOT

(*Laughs*)

My God, think of you having a priest for an uncle! That's too rich!

JOHN

I haven't seen him since I was a boy.

ELIOT

Why so scared? Afraid he's come to lecture you on your sins?

LOVING

(*Angrily*)

He may be a joke to you. He's not to me, damn him!

ELIOT

(*Gives* JOHN *a surprised, disapproving glance*)

Oh, come, John. Not as bad as that, is it? He struck me as a nice old guy.

JOHN

(*Hurriedly*)

He is. I didn't mean that. I always liked him. He was very kind to me when I was a kid. He acted as my guardian for a while. But I wish he'd given me warning. (*Then picking up the telephone*) Well, it's rotten to keep him cooling his heels. Hello. Send Father Baird in.

ELIOT

(*Turning to the door*)

I'll get out.

DAYS WITHOUT END

No, as a favor, stay around until the ice is broken. (*He has gotten up and is going toward the door.* LOVING *remains in his chair, his eyes fixed before him in a hostile stare, his body tensed defensively.*)

ELIOT

Sure. (*A knock comes on the door.* JOHN *opens it and* FATHER MATTHEW BAIRD *enters. He is seventy, about* JOHN *and* LOVING'S *height, erect, robust, with thick white hair, ruddy complexion. There is a clear resemblance to* JOHN *and* LOVING *in the general cast of his features and the color of his eyes. His appearance and personality radiate health and observant kindliness—also the confident authority of one who is accustomed to obedience and deference—and one gets immediately from him the sense of an unshakable inner calm and certainty, the peace of one whose goal in life is fixed by an end beyond life.*)

JOHN
(*Constrained and at the same time affectionate*)
Hello, Uncle! What in the world brings you—

FATHER BAIRD
(*Clasping* JOHN'S *hand in a strong grip*)
Jack! (*His manner is very much what it must have been when* JOHN *was a boy and he was the guardian. Deeply moved, he puts his arm around* JOHN *and gives him an affectionate hug*) My dear Jack! This is— (*He sees* ELIOT *and stops, a bit embarrassed.*)

29

JOHN

(*Moved and embarrassed, getting away from his arm*)

I want you to meet my partner—Bill Eliot—my uncle, Father Baird.

ELIOT

It's a great pleasure, Father.

FATHER BAIRD

(*Shakes his hand—a formal, old-fashioned courtesy in his manner*)

The pleasure is mine, Mr. Eliot. But I feel I've had the privilege of your acquaintance already through Jack's letters.

JOHN

Sit down, Uncle. (*He indicates the chair at right of desk.* FATHER BAIRD *sits down.* JOHN *sits in his chair at left.* ELIOT *stands by the chair at right, center.*)

ELIOT

Well, I'll leave you two alone and pretend to be busy. That's the hardest job we have now, Father—keeping up the pretense of work.

FATHER BAIRD

You have plenty of company, if that's any consolation. I get the same tale of woe from every one in our part of the country.

ELIOT

I'm afraid the company doesn't console a bit. They're all too darned whiney.

30

FATHER BAIRD

(*A twinkle coming into his eye*)

Ah, who can blame you for whining when your omnipotent Golden Calf explodes into sawdust before your adoring eyes right at the height of his deification? It's tragic, no other word —unless the word be comic.

LOVING

(*His voice a mocking sneer*)

And what salvation for us are you preaching? The Second Coming?

FATHER BAIRD

(*Startled, turns to stare at* JOHN. ELIOT *also looks at him, surprised and disapproving of this taunt.* FATHER BAIRD *says quietly, without any sign of taking offense*)

The First Coming is enough, Jack—for those who remember it. (*Then he turns to* ELIOT—*in a joking tone*) If you knew how familiar that note sounds from him, Mr. Eliot. Here I've been feeling strange, looking at him and seeing what a big man of affairs he'd grown, and saying to myself, can this be my old Jack? And then he has to go and give himself away with a strain of his old bold whistling in the dark, and I see he's still only out of short pants a while, as I knew him last! (*He gives a comic sigh of relief*) Thank you, Jack. I feel quite at home with you now.

ELIOT

(*Immensely amused, especially at the expression of boyish discomfiture on* JOHN's *face—laughingly*)

John, I begin to feel sorry for you. You've picked on some one out of your class.

DAYS WITHOUT END

FATHER BAIRD

(*With a wink at* ELIOT)

Did you hear him throw the word preaching in my face, Mr. Eliot—with a dirty sneer in his voice? There's injustice for you. If you knew what a burden he made my life for years with his preaching. Letter upon letter—each with a soap box inclosed, so to speak. The plague began right after I'd had to go West and leave him to his own devices. He was about to pass out of my guardianship and go to college with the bit of money his parents had left for him when he reached eighteen. So I had to let him go his own way. I'd learned it was no use fighting him, anyway. I'd done that and found it was a great satisfaction to him and only made him worse. And I had faith, if let alone, he'd come back to his senses in the end.

LOVING

(*Sneeringly*)

And how mistaken you were in that faith!

FATHER BAIRD

(*Without turning—quietly*)

No. The end isn't yet, Jack. (*He goes on to* ELIOT *with a renewal of his humorously complaining tone*) You wouldn't believe what a devil's advocate he was in those days, Mr. Eliot.

ELIOT

You needn't tell me, Father. I was his classmate. He organized an Atheists' Club—or tried to—and almost got fired for it.

32

DAYS WITHOUT END

Yes, I remember his writing to boast about that. Well, you can appreciate then what I went through, even if he didn't write you letters.

ELIOT

But he delivered harangues, Father, when he could get anybody to listen!

FATHER BAIRD

(*Pityingly*)

Ah, that must have been cruel, too. Mr. Eliot, I feel drawn to you. We've been through the same frightful trials.

JOHN

(*With a boyishly discomfited air*)

I hope you're having a good time, you two.

FATHER BAIRD

(*Ignoring him*)

Not a moment's peace did he give me. I was the heathen to him and he was bound he'd convert me to something. First it was Atheism unadorned. Then it was Atheism wedded to Socialism. But Socialism proved too weak-kneed a mate, and the next I heard Atheism was living in free love with Anarchism, with a curse by Nietzsche to bless the union. And then came the Bolshevik dawn, and he greeted that with unholy howls of glee and wrote me he'd found a congenial home at last in the bosom of Karl Marx. He was particularly delighted when he thought they'd abolished love and marriage, and he couldn't contain himself when the news came they'd turned naughty schoolboys and were throwing spit-balls at Almighty God and had supplanted Him with the

33

slave-owning State—the most grotesque god that ever came out of Asia!

ELIOT

(*Chuckling*)

I recognize all this, Father. I used to read his articles, as I was reminding him just before you came.

FATHER BAIRD

Don't I know them! Didn't he send me every one with blue pencil underlinings! But to get back to my story: Thinks I at this juncture, well, he's run away as far as he can get in that direction. Where will he hide himself next?

LOVING

(*Stiffening in his chair—with angry resentment*)

Run away? You talk as if I were afraid of something. Hide? Hide from what?

FATHER BAIRD

(*Without turning—quietly*)

Don't you know, Jack? Well, if you don't yet, you will some day. (*Again to* ELIOT) I knew Communism wouldn't hold him long—and it didn't. Soon his letters became full of pessimism, and disgust with all sociological nostrums. Then followed a long silence. And what do you think was his next hiding place? Religion, no less—but as far away as he could run from home—in the defeatist mysticism of the East. First it was China and Lao Tze that fascinated him, but afterwards he ran on to Buddha, and his letters for a time extolled passionless contemplation so passionately that I had a mental view of him regarding his navel frenziedly by the hour and making nothing

34

of it! (ELIOT *laughs and* JOHN *chuckles sheepishly in spite of himself.* LOVING *stares before him with a cold, angry disdain.*)

ELIOT

Gosh, I'm sorry I missed that! When was all this, Father?

FATHER BAIRD

In what I'd call his middle hide-and-go-seek period. But the next I knew, he was through with the East. It was not for the Western soul, he decided, and he was running through Greek philosophy and found a brief shelter in Pythagoras and numerology. Then came a letter which revealed him bogged down in evolutionary scientific truth again—a dyed-in-the-wool mechanist. That was the last I heard of his perigrinations—and, thank heaven, it was long ago. I enjoyed a long interval of peace from his missionary zeal, until finally he wrote me he was married. That letter was full of more ardent hymns of praise for a mere living woman than he'd ever written before about any of his great spiritual discoveries. And ever since then I've heard nothing but the praises of Elsa—in which I know I'll be ready to join after I've met her.

JOHN
(*His face lighting up*)
You bet you will! We can agree on that, at least.

FATHER BAIRD
(*With a wink at* ELIOT)
He seems to be fixed in his last religion. I hope so. The only constant faith I've found in him before was his proud belief in himself as a bold Antichrist. (*He gives* JOHN *a side glance, half smiling and half reproachful*) Ah well, it's a rocky road,

full of twists and blind alleys, isn't it, Jack—this running away from truth in order to find it? I mean, until the road finally turns back toward home.

LOVING

(*With harsh defiance*)

You believe I—? (*Then sneeringly*) But, of course, you would read that into it.

JOHN

(*Bursts out irritably, as if he couldn't control his nerves*)

But don't you think I'm about exhausted as a subject, Uncle? I do. (*He gets up nervously and moves around and stands behind* LOVING's *chair, his hands on the back of the chair, his face directly above* LOVING's *masked one.*)

ELIOT

(*Gives the priest an amused smile*)

Well, I'll get back to my office. (FATHER BAIRD *gets up and he shakes his hand heartily*) I hope we'll meet again, Father. Are you here for long?

FATHER BAIRD

Only a few days, I'm afraid.

JOHN

(*Coming around to them*)

I'll fix up something with Elsa for the four of us, Bill—as soon as she's feeling stronger. We won't let him run away in a few days, now we've got him here.

DAYS WITHOUT END

ELIOT

Fine! See you again, then, Father. (*He goes toward the door.*)

FATHER BAIRD

I hope so, Mr. Eliot. Good day to you.

ELIOT

(*With the door open, turns back with a grin*)

I feel it my duty, Father, to warn you that John's got writer's itch again. He's going to give us a novel. (*He laughs and closes the door behind him.* JOHN *frowns and gives his uncle a quick uneasy glance.*)

JOHN

(*Indicating the chair at right, center*)

Take that chair, Uncle. It's more comfortable. (*He sits down in the chair at right of table where* FATHER BAIRD *had sat, while the priest sits in the one at right, center.* FATHER BAIRD *gives him a puzzled, concerned look, as if he were trying to figure something out. Then he speaks casually.*)

FATHER BAIRD

A novel? Is that right, Jack?

JOHN

(*Without looking at him*)

Thinking of it—to pass the time.

FATHER BAIRD

Then, judging from your letters, it ought to be a love story.

JOHN

It is—a love story.

37

LOVING

(Mockingly)

About God's love for us!

FATHER BAIRD

(Quietly rebuking)

Jack! (*A pause of silence.* FATHER BAIRD *gives* JOHN *a quick glance again—then casually*) If you've any appointments, don't stand on ceremony; just shoo me out.

JOHN

(Turns to him shamefacedly)

Don't talk that way, Uncle. You know I wouldn't—(*with a natural, boyishly affectionate smile*) You know darned well how tickled I am to have you here.

FATHER BAIRD

I hope you're half as glad as I am to see you, Jack. (*He sighs*) It has been a long time—too long.

JOHN

Yes. (*Smiling*) But I'm still flabbergasted. I never dreamed you— Why didn't you wire me you were coming?

FATHER BAIRD

Oh, I thought I'd surprise you. (*He smiles*) To tell you the truth, I confess I had a sneaking Sherlock Holmes desire to have a good look at you before you were expecting it.

JOHN

(Frowning—uneasily)

Why? Why should you?

DAYS WITHOUT END

FATHER BAIRD

Well, I suppose because, not having seen you, I'm afraid that to me you were still the boy I'd known, and I was still your suspicious guardian.

JOHN

(Relieved—with a boyish grin)

Oh! I see.

FATHER BAIRD

And now I have seen you, I still must admit that the gray in your hair is lost on me, and I can't get it out of my head you're the same old Jack.

JOHN

(Grinning with a boyish discomfiture)

Yes, and the devil of it is you make me feel that way, too. It's an unfair advantage, Uncle. (FATHER BAIRD *laughs and* JOHN *joins in.*)

FATHER BAIRD

Well, I never took unfair advantage of you in the old days, did I?

JOHN

You certainly didn't. When I look back, I'm amazed you could have been so fair. *(Quickly—changing the subject)* But you haven't told me yet how you happened to come East.

FATHER BAIRD

(A bit evasively)

Oh, I decided a vacation was due me. And I've had a great longing for some time to see you again.

JOHN

I only wish I could have you stay with us, but there's no room. But you must have dinner with us to-night, and every night you're here, of course.

FATHER BAIRD

Yes, I'd like to see all of you I can. But there's this, Jack. You spoke to Mr. Eliot as if Elsa were ill.

JOHN

Oh, it's nothing serious. She's just getting over the flu, and still feels a bit low.

FATHER BAIRD

Then I'd better not come to-night.

JOHN

You better had or she'll never forgive you—or me!

FATHER BAIRD

Very well. I'm only too happy. (*A pause. He glances at* JOHN *again with a curious puzzled fixity.* JOHN *catches his eyes, is held by them for a moment, then looks away almost furtively.*)

JOHN

(*Forcing a smile*)

Is that the suspicious guardian look? I've forgotten.

FATHER BAIRD

(*As if to himself—slowly*)

I feel— (*Then suddenly*) There's something I want to tell you, Jack. (*A stern note comes into his voice*) But first give me your word of honor there will be no cheap sneering.

JOHN

(*Stares at him, taken aback—then quietly*)

There won't be.

FATHER BAIRD

Well, it's often come to me in the past that I shouldn't have let you get so far from me, that I might be in part responsible for your continued estrangement from your Faith.

LOVING

(*With mocking scorn*)

My faith?

JOHN

You know that's nonsense, Uncle.

LOVING

You have always nobly done your duty. You've never let a letter pass without some pious reminder of my fall—with the calm assurance that I would again see the light. That never failed to make me laugh—your complacent assumption that like the Prodigal of His fairy tale, I—

FATHER BAIRD

(*Sharply*)

Jack! You promised!

JOHN

(*Confusedly*)

I know. I didn't mean— Go on with what you started to tell me.

FATHER BAIRD

First answer me frankly one question. Have you been greatly troubled in spirit by anything lately?

JOHN

(*Startled*)

I? Why do you ask that? Of course not. (*Then evasively*) Oh, well—yes, maybe, if you mean business worries.

FATHER BAIRD

Nothing else?

JOHN

No. What could there be?

FATHER BAIRD

(*Unconvinced—looking away*)

The reason I asked— You'll see in what I'm going to tell you. It happened one night while I was praying for you in my church, as I have every day since I left you. A strange feeling of fear took possession of me—a feeling you were unhappy, in some great spiritual danger. I told myself it was foolish. I'd had a letter from you only that day, reiterating how happy you were. I tried to lose my dread in prayer—and my guilt. Yes, I felt stricken with guilt, too—that I was to blame for whatever was happening to you. Then, as I prayed, suddenly as if by some will outside me, my eyes were drawn to the Cross, to the face of Our Blessed Lord. And it was like a miracle! His face seemed alive as a living man's would be, but radiant with eternal life, too, especially the sad, pitying eyes. But there was a sternness in His eyes, too, an accusation against me—a command about you! (*He breaks off and gives* JOHN *a quick glance, as if afraid of finding him sneering. Then, looking away, he adds simply*) That's the real reason I decided to take my vacation in the East, Jack.

42

JOHN
(Stares at him fascinatedly)

You saw—?

LOVING
(In a bitter, sneering tone)

It could hardly have been any concern for me you saw in His face—even if He did exist or ever had existed!

FATHER BAIRD
(Sternly)

Jack! *(Then, after a pause, quietly)* Do you know Francis Thompson's poem—The Hound of Heaven?

LOVING

I did once. Why?

FATHER BAIRD
(Quotes in a low voice but with deep feeling)

"Ah, fondest, blindest, weakest,
I am He Whom thou seekest!
Thou dravest love from thee, who dravest Me."

LOVING
(In what is close to a snarl of scorn)

Love!

JOHN
(Defensively)

I have love!

FATHER BAIRD
(As if he hadn't heard)

Why do you run and hide from Him, as from an enemy? Take care. There comes a time in every man's life when he

43

must have his God for friend, or he has no friend at all, not even himself. Who knows? Perhaps you are on the threshold of that time now.

JOHN

(*Uneasily*)

What do you mean?

FATHER BAIRD

I don't know. It's for you to know that. You say you have love?

JOHN

You know I have. Or, if you don't, you soon will after you've met Elsa.

FATHER BAIRD

I'm not doubting your love for her nor hers for you. It's exactly because I do not doubt. I am thinking that such love needs the hope and promise of eternity to fulfill itself—above all, to feel itself secure. Beyond the love for each other should be the love of God, in Whose Love yours may find the triumph over death.

LOVING

(*Sneeringly*)

Old superstition, born of fear! Beyond death there is nothing. That, at least, is certain—a certainty we should be thankful for. One life is boring enough. Do not condemn us to another. Let us rest in peace at last!

FATHER BAIRD

(*Quietly*)

Would you talk that way if Elsa should die?

DAYS WITHOUT END

JOHN

(*With a shudder*)

For God's sake, don't speak about—

LOVING

Do you think I haven't imagined her death many times?

JOHN

The dread of it has haunted me ever since we were married.

FATHER BAIRD

Ah.

LOVING

You'll see that I face it—by proxy, at least—in my novel. (*A sneering taunt in his voice*) I think you'll be interested in this novel, Uncle.

FATHER BAIRD

(*Staring at* JOHN, *whose face is averted*)

It's autobiographical, then?

JOHN

(*Hastily*)

No. Of course not. I only meant— Don't get that idea in your head, for Pete's sake. As I explained to Elsa, when I told her about the first part, it's really the story of a man I once knew.

LOVING

The first part will particularly interest you, Uncle. I am afraid you will be terribly shocked—especially in the light of your recent mystic vision!

45

FATHER BAIRD

I'm very curious to hear it, Jack. When will you tell me?

LOVING

(*Defiantly*)

Now!

JOHN

(*Uneasily*)

But no. I don't want to bore you.

FATHER BAIRD

You won't bore me.

JOHN

No— I—

LOVING

(*With harsh insistence*)

The first part concerns my hero's boyhood here in New York, up to the age of fifteen.

JOHN

(*Under* LOVING's *compulsion, he picks up the thread of the story*)

He was an only child. His father was a fine man. The boy adored him. And he adored his mother even more. She was a wonderful woman, a perfect type of our old beautiful ideal of wife and mother.

LOVING

(*Sneeringly*)

But there was one ridiculous weakness in her character, an absurd obsession with religion. In the father's, too. They were both devout Catholics.

46

DAYS WITHOUT END

(*The priest gives a swift, reproachful look at* JOHN, *seems about to protest, thinks better of it, and drops his eyes.*)

JOHN
(*Quickly*)

But not the ignorant, bigoted sort, please understand. No, their piety had a genuine, gentle, mystic quality to it. Their faith was the great comforting inspiration of their lives. And their God was One of Infinite Love—not a stern, self-righteous Being Who condemned sinners to torment, but a very human, lovable God Who became man for love of men and gave His life that they might be saved from themselves. And the boy had every reason to believe in such a Divinity of Love as the Creator of Life. His home atmosphere was one of love. Life *was* love for him then. And he was happy, happier than he ever afterward— (*He checks himself abruptly.*)

FATHER BAIRD
(*Nods his head approvingly*)

Yes.

JOHN

Later, at school, he learned of the God of Punishment, and he wondered. He couldn't reconcile Him with his parents' faith. So it didn't make much impression on him.

LOVING
(*Bitterly*)

Then! But afterward he had good reason to—

JOHN

But then he was too sure in his faith. He grew up as devout

47

as his parents. He even dreamed of becoming a priest. He used to love to kneel in the church before the Cross.

LOVING

Oh, he was a remarkably superstitious young fool! (*His voice suddenly changes to hard bitterness*) And then when he was fifteen, all these pious illusions of his were destroyed forever! Both his parents were killed!

JOHN

(*Hurriedly*)

That is, they died during a flu epidemic in which they contracted pneumonia—and he was left alone—without love. First, his father died. The boy had prayed with perfect faith that his father's life might be spared.

LOVING

But his father died! And the poor simpleton's naïve faith was a bit shaken, and a sinful doubt concerning the Divine Love assailed him!

JOHN

Then his mother, worn out by nursing his father and by her grief, was taken ill. And the horrible fear came to him that she might die, too.

LOVING

It drove the young idiot into a panic of superstitious remorse. He imagined her sickness was a terrible warning to him, a punishment for the doubt inspired in him by his father's death. (*With harsh bitterness*) His God of Love was beginning to show Himself as a God of Vengeance, you see!

48

JOHN

But he still trusted in His Love. Surely He would not take his mother from him, too.

LOVING

So the poor fool prayed and prayed and vowed his life to piety and good works! But he began to make a condition now—*if* his mother were spared to him!

JOHN

Finally he knew in his heart she was going to die. But even then he hoped and prayed for a miracle.

LOVING

He abased and humbled himself before the Cross—and, in reward for his sickening humiliation, saw that no miracle would happen.

JOHN

Something snapped in him then.

LOVING

(*His voice suddenly takes on a tone of bitter hatred*)
He saw his God as deaf and blind and merciless—a Deity Who returned hate for love and revenged Himself upon those who trusted Him!

JOHN

His mother died. And, in a frenzy of insane grief—

LOVING

No! In his awakened pride he cursed his God and denied Him, and, in revenge, promised his soul to the Devil—on his knees, when every one thought he was praying! (*He laughs with malignant bitterness.*)

49

JOHN

(*Quickly—in a casual tone*)

And that's the end of Part One, as I've outlined it.

FATHER BAIRD

(*Horrified*)

Jack! I can't believe that you—

JOHN

(*Defensively*)

I? What have I to do with it? You're forgetting I explained to you— Oh, I admit there are certain points of resemblance between some of his boyhood experiences and mine—his parents' death, for example. But that's only coincidence.

FATHER BAIRD

(*Recovered now—staring at him—quietly*)

I see.

JOHN

(*Forcing a smile*)

And please don't bring up those coincidences before Elsa, Uncle. She didn't notice them because I've never bored her with boyhood reminiscences. And I don't want her to get the wrong angle on my plot.

FATHER BAIRD

I'll remember, Jack. When will you tell me the rest of it?

JOHN

Oh, some time while you're here, maybe.

FATHER BAIRD

Why not to-night at your home?

JOHN

Well, I might—

LOVING

That is, if I can decide on my end before then!

JOHN

It would give me a chance to get your and Elsa's criticisms at the same time. She's been wanting to hear the rest of it, too.

FATHER BAIRD

(*Regarding him—quietly*)

Then, by all means. (*Abruptly changing to a brisk casualness*) Well, I'll leave you and attend to some errand I have to do. (*He gets to his feet. He takes* JOHN'S *hand.*)

JOHN

Dinner is at seven-thirty. But come as long before that as you like. I'll be home early. (*Then with a genuine boyish affection*) I want to tell you again, Uncle, how grand it is to have you here—in spite of our arguments.

FATHER BAIRD

I'm not worried by our arguments. But I am about something about you that admits of no argument—to me.

JOHN

(*Forcing a smile*)

You're wasting worry. But what is it?

FATHER BAIRD

You've written me you were happy, and I believed you. But, now I see you, I don't believe you. You're not happy. Why? Perhaps if you had it out with me—

LOVING
(*Mockingly*)

Confess, eh?

JOHN

Don't be foolish, Uncle. I am happy, happier than I ever dreamed I could be. And, for heaven's sake, don't go telling Elsa I'm unhappy!

FATHER BAIRD
(*Quietly*)

Very well. We'll say no more about it. And now I'll be off. Good-bye until this evening, Jack.

JOHN

So long, Uncle. (FATHER BAIRD *goes out.* JOHN *stands by the door, looking after him—then he comes slowly back and sits down in his chair and stares before him.* LOVING's *eyes are fastened on him with a cold contempt.*)

LOVING

Damned old fool with his bedtime tales for second childhood about the love of God! And you—you're worse—with your hypocritical lies about your great happiness!

(*The telephone on the table rings.* JOHN *jumps nervously —then answers it in an apprehensive voice.*)

JOHN

Hello. Who? Tell her I'm out.

LOVING

You'd better find out what she wants.

52

JOHN

No, wait. I'll take it. (*Then, his voice becoming guarded and pleasantly casual*) Hello, Lucy. Bill told me you'd called. What—? (*He listens—then anxiety creeping into his tone*) She phoned again? What about? Oh. I'm glad you called me. Yes, she has been wondering why she hasn't heard from you in so long. Yes, by all means, go. Yes, she's sure to be in this afternoon. Good-bye. (*He hangs up mechanically.*)

LOVING

(*Sneeringly*)

Your terrible sin begins to close in on you, eh? But then, it wasn't you, was it? It was some evil spirit that possessed you! (*He gives a mocking laugh—then stops abruptly and continues in his tone of cold, sinister insistence*) But enough of that nonsense. Let's return to your plot. The wife dies—of influenza that turns into pneumonia, let's say.

JOHN

(*Starts violently—stammers*)

What—God damn you—what makes you choose that?

Curtain

ACT TWO

PLOT FOR A NOVEL

(*Continued*)

ACT TWO

SCENE—*The living-room of the* LOVINGS' *duplex apartment. Venetian blinds soften the light from a big window at right. In front of this window is a table with a lamp. At left, front, an upholstered chair. At right of chair, a small table with a lamp. At right of table, in the center of the room, a sofa. In front of sofa, a low stand with cigarette box and ash trays. Toward right, another chair. In the left wall is a door leading to the dining-room. At rear of door, a writing desk. In the middle of the rear wall is a doorway leading to the hall.*

It is later the same afternoon.

ELSA *enters from the hall at rear. She is thirty-five but looks much younger. She is beautiful with that Indian Summer renewal of physical charm which comes to a woman who loves and is loved, particularly to one who has not found that love until comparatively late in life. This beauty is a trifle dimmed now by traces of recent illness. Her face is drawn and she fights against a depressing lassitude. She wears a simple negligée.*

As she comes in, she presses a button by the door and a buzzer is heard in the pantry. She comes forward and sits on the sofa. A moment later MARGARET, *the maid, appears from the dining-room at left. She is a middle-aged Irishwoman with a kindly face.*

MARGARET

Yes, Madame?

ELSA

Hasn't the afternoon paper come yet, Margaret?

MARGARET

No, Madame, not yet. (*Then with kindly reproof*) Didn't you take a nap like you promised you would?

ELSA

I couldn't get to sleep. But I do feel rested, so don't begin to scold me. (*She smiles and* MARGARET *smiles back, a look of devoted affection lighting up her face.*)

MARGARET

You have to take care. The flu's a bad thing the way it leaves you weak after. And you're only out of your bed two days.

ELSA

Oh, I'm really quite well again. And I was too excited to sleep. I kept thinking of Mr. Loving's uncle. (*The telephone in the hall rings and* MARGARET *goes toward the door in rear to answer it.*) Heavens, I hope that isn't he now. Mr. Loving phoned me he told him to come early. But surely he wouldn't this early!

MARGARET

(*Disappears in the hall. Her voice comes*)
Just a moment and I'll see if she's in. (*She appears again in the doorway*) It's Mrs. Hillman calling to see you, Madame.

DAYS WITHOUT END

ELSA

Oh, I'm glad. Tell her to come right up. (MARGARET *disappears and is heard relaying this instruction. Then she appears in the hall outside the doorway, waiting to answer the door.* ELSA *speaks to her*) I wish I didn't look so like a sick cat. Why is it every one decides to turn up when you look your worst?

MARGARET

Ah, you needn't worry, Madame. You look fine.

ELSA

Well, anyway, I don't mind Lucy. (*Nevertheless, she goes to the desk at left, rear, takes out a vanity case, powders her nose, etc. While she is doing this,* MARGARET *moves to the entrance door in the hall and is heard admitting* MRS. HILLMAN *and exchanging greetings with her, as she helps her off with her things.* ELSA *calls*) Hello, Stranger.

LUCY

(*Calls back in a voice whose breeziness rings a bit strained*)

That's right, sit on me the minute I set foot in your house! Well, I know I deserve it. (ELSA *goes to the doorway and meets her as she comes in, kissing her affectionately.* LUCY HILLMAN *is about the same age as* ELSA. *She is still an extremely attractive woman but, in contrast to* ELSA, *her age shows, in spite of a heavy make-up. There are wrinkles about her eyes, and her small, full, rather weak mouth is drawn down by sharp lines at the corners. She is dressed expensively in clothes a bit too youthful and extreme in style. She responds to* ELSA'S *greeting with a nervous constraint*) Hello, Elsa.

59

ELSA

You're a nice one! How long has it been—months!—not since before I went to Boston in February. (*She sits on the sofa and draws* LUCY *down beside her.*)

LUCY

I know. I'm in the dust at your feet.

ELSA

I've phoned you a dozen times, but you were always out. Or did you just tell them to say that? I've completely lost faith in you.

LUCY

But I was out, Elsa. How can you think—

ELSA

(*Laughing—gives her a hug*)

You're not taking me seriously, are you? I know you'd hardly do that with me, after all these years.

LUCY

Of course, I wouldn't.

ELSA

But I did wonder a little at your sudden complete ignoring of our existence. So did John.

LUCY

(*Hurriedly*)

If you know all the stupid engagements that pile up—and all the idiotic parties Walter lets me in for. (*Then changing the subject abruptly*) May I have a cigarette? (*She takes one from the box on the stand and lights it*) Aren't you having one?

ELSA

Not now. (*She gives* LUCY *a puzzled glance.* LUCY *avoids her eyes, nervously flipping her cigarette over the ash tray.* ELSA *asks*) How are the kids?

LUCY

Oh, fine, thanks. At least, I think so, from the little I get to see of them nowadays. (*Bitterness has crept into this last. She again hurriedly changes the subject*) But tell me all your news. What have you been doing with yourself?

ELSA

Oh, the same peaceful routine—going to a concert now and then, reading a lot, keeping house, taking care of John.

LUCY

The old perfect marriage that's been the wonder of us all, eh? (*Again changing the subject*) What time does John usually get home? I don't want to run into him.

ELSA

Oh, not for an hour or so yet. (*Smiling*) But why? What have you got against John?

LUCY

(*Smiling with a strange wryness*)

Nothing—except myself. (*Then hurriedly*) I mean, look at me, I look like hell. I've had the damndest insomnia lately. And I'm vain enough not to crave any male viewing the wreckage until I've spruced up on a bath and cocktails.

ELSA

But that's silly. You look wonderful.

LUCY

(*Dryly*)

Thanks, liar! (*With a side glance of frank envy—unable to keep resentment out of her voice*) I especially don't care to be up for inspection beside you. The contrast is too glaring.

ELSA

But it's I who look like the devil, not you. I'm just getting over flu.

LUCY

Flu makes no never mind. It doesn't affect—what I mean. (*Then with a hard flippant air*) Pardon me if I seem to indulge in the melancholy jitters. I'm becoming the damndest whiner and self-pitier. It's really too boring. (*She lights another cigarette. Her hands have a nervous tremor.* ELSA *watches her with a worried, affectionately pitying look.*)

ELSA

What is it, Lucy? Tell me.

LUCY

(*Stiffening defensively*)

What is what?

ELSA

I want to know what's troubling you. Now, there's no use denying it. I've known you too long. I felt it the moment you

62

came in, that you were upset about something and trying to hide it.

LUCY

I don't know where you got that idea. (*Defensively flippant*) Oh, really now, Elsa. Don't you go psychic on us!

ELSA

All right, then. Forgive my trying to pump you. But you got me into the bad habit yourself, you know, by always coming to me with your troubles. I only thought I might be able to help.

LUCY

You! (*She gives a hard little laugh.*)

ELSA

(*Hurt*)

You used to think I could.

LUCY

"Once, long ago—" (*Then, suddenly with repentant shame-facedness*) Forgive me, Elsa. I'm rotten to be flip about that. You've been the most wonderful friend. And I'm such an ungrateful little slut!

ELSA

Lucy! You mustn't say that.

LUCY

(*Hurries on with a simulation of frankness*)

But honestly, you're mistaken this time. There's nothing wrong, except what seems to be wrong with every one, the stupid lives we lead—and, of course, the usual financial worries. So please don't bother your head about my troubles.

ELSA

All right, dear. (*Then, after a slight pause—casually*) How is Walter these days?

LUCY

(*With a twisted smile*)

I thought we weren't going to talk about my troubles! Oh, Walter is—Walter. You know him, Elsa. Why ask? But do you know any one, I wonder? Darned if I think you ever see what people really are. You somehow manage to live in some lost world where human beings are still decent and honorable. I don't see how you do it. If you'd always been a little innocent, protected from all ugly contacts— But, my God, your first marriage must have slapped your face with about every filthy thing a man can be—and that's plenty! Yet you sit here, calm and beautiful and unscarred—!

ELSA

(*Quietly*)

I have my share of scars. But the wounds are all healed—completely healed. John's love has done that for me.

LUCY

Yes—of course. (*Then, as if she couldn't control herself, she bursts out*) Oh, you and your John! You bring him up as the answer to everything.

ELSA

(*Smiling*)

Well, he is for me.

64

LUCY

Do you mean to tell me you're as much in love with him now as when you married him?

ELSA

Oh, much more so, for he's become my child and father now, as well as being a husband and—

LUCY

Lover. Say it. How incredibly Mid-Victorian you can be! Don't you know that's all we married ladies discuss nowadays? But you're lucky. Usually the men discussed aren't our husbands, and aren't even good lovers. But never say die. We keep on hoping and experimenting!

ELSA

(*Repelled*)

Don't talk in that disgusting way. I know you don't mean a word of it.

LUCY

(*Stares at her resentfully for a second, then turns away, reaching for another cigarette—dryly*)

Oh, you're quite sure of that, are you?

ELSA

(*Gently*)

Lucy, what is it has made you so bitter? I've noticed it growing on you for the past few years, but now it's completely got you. I—honestly, I hardly know you this time, you've changed so.

65

LUCY

(*Hurriedly*)

Oh, it's nothing that happened lately. You mustn't get that idea. (*Then letting herself go—with increasing bitterness*) It's simply that I've grown sick of my life, sick of all the lying and faking of it, sick of marriage and motherhood, sick of myself! Particularly sick of myself because I endure the humiliation of Walter's open affairs with every damned floosie he meets! And I'm tired of pretending I don't mind, tired of really minding underneath, tired of pretending to myself I have to go on for the children's sakes, and that they make up to me for everything, which they don't at all!

ELSA

(*Indignantly*)

How can Walter be such a beast!

LUCY

(*With a look at* ELSA *that is almost vindictive*)

Oh, he's no worse than a lot of others. At least, he doesn't lie about it.

ELSA

But, for heaven's sake, why do you stand it? Why don't you leave him?

LUCY

Oh, don't be so superior and scornful, Elsa. I'll bet you wouldn't— (*She checks herself abruptly.*)

ELSA

What do you mean? You know very well I left my first husband the minute I found out—

66

DAYS WITHOUT END

LUCY

(*Hurriedly*)

I know. I didn't— Why don't I leave Walter? I guess because I'm too worn out to have the guts. And then I did try it once. The first time I knew he'd been unfaithful I did the correct thing and went home. I intended to tell Father I was through as Walter's wife. Only Father was away. Mother was there, and I broke down and told her. She took it quite philosophically—said I was a fool to expect too much, men were like that, even my father had— (*She gives a little shiver of aversion*) That sort of squelched me. So I went back to Walter and he doesn't know to this day I ever left him.

ELSA

I'm so sorry, Lucy.

LUCY

(*Returning to her air of hard cynicism*)

No pity, please. After all, the situation has its compensations. He has tried nobly to be fair. He said I could have equal liberty to indulge any of my sexual whims.

ELSA

What a stupid fool!

LUCY

(*Bitterly*)

Oh, he didn't really mean it, you know. His vanity couldn't admit I'd ever feel the slightest desire outside of him. It was only a silly gesture he felt safe in making because he was so damned sure of me—because he knows, damn him, that in spite of all he's done to kill it there's still a cowardly slavish something in me, dating back to the happiness of our first married days, which still—loves him! (*She starts to break down, but fights this back and bursts out vindictively, a look of ugly satisfaction coming into her face*) But I warned him he'd humiliate me once too often—and he did!

ELSA
(*Shocked*)

You mean you—

LUCY
(*With a return of her flippant tone*)

Yes, I went in for a little fleeting adultery. And I must say, as a love substitute or even a pleasurable diversion, it's greatly overrated. (*She gives a hard little laugh*) How horribly shocked you look! Are you going to order me from your virtuous home?

ELSA

Lucy! Don't talk like that! It's only that I can't believe—none of this is really you. That's what makes it so— But please don't think I'm condemning you. You know how I love you, don't you?

LUCY
(*Stares at her with a strange panic*)

Don't, for God's sake! I don't want you to love me! I'd rather you hated me! (*But* ELSA *pulls her to her and she breaks down finally, sobbing, her face buried against* ELSA's *shoulder.*)

ELSA

There, there. You mustn't, dear. (*Then as* LUCY *grows calmer —quietly*) Don't think I don't understand, because I do. I felt

68

exactly the same when I found out about Ned Howell. Even though I'd stopped caring for him and our marriage had always been unhappy, my pride was so hurt I wanted to revenge myself and take the first man I met for a lover.

LUCY

(*Looks up in amazement*)
You went through that? I never dreamed—

ELSA

All that saved me from doing something stupid was the faith I had that somewhere the man was waiting whom I could really love. I felt I owed it to him and to my own self-respect not to deliberately disfigure myself out of wounded pride and spite.

LUCY

(*With sad bitterness*)
You hit it when you say disfigure. That's how I've felt ever since. Cheap! Ugly! As if *I'd* deliberately disfigured *myself*. And not only myself—the man—and others I wouldn't hurt for anything in the world—if I was in my right mind. But I wasn't! You realize I wasn't, don't you, Elsa? You must! You above every one!

ELSA

I do, dear. Of course I do.

LUCY

I've got to tell you just how it came to happen—so you'll see. It was one of Walter's parties. You know the would-be Bohemian gang he likes to have. They were there in all their vulgarity, their poisonous, envious tongues wise-cracking at everything with any decent human dignity and worth. Oh,

69

there were a few others there, too—our own people—this man was one of them. Walter was drunk, pawing over his latest female, and she got him to go home with her. Everybody watched me to see how I'd take it. I wanted to kill him and her, but I only laughed and had some more to drink. But I was in hell, I can tell you, and inside I kept swearing to myself that I'd show Walter— And I picked out this man—yes, deliberately! It was all deliberate and crazy! And I had to do all the seducing—because he's quite happy. I knew that, but I was crazy. His happiness filled me with rage—the thought that he made others happy. I wanted to take his happiness from him and kill it as mine had been killed!

ELSA

Lucy!

LUCY

(*With a hard laugh*)

I told you I was in hell, didn't I? You can't live there without becoming like the rest of the crowd! (*Hurrying on with her story*) I got him in my bedroom on some excuse. But he pushed me away, as if he were disgusted with himself and me. But I wouldn't let him go. And then came the strange part of it. Suddenly, I don't know how to explain it, you'll think I'm crazy, or being funny, but it was as if he were no longer there. It was another man, a stranger whose eyes were hateful and frightening. He seemed to look through me at some one else, and I seemed for a moment to be watching some hidden place in his mind where there was something as evil and revengeful as I was. It frightened and fascinated me—and called to me too; that's the hell of it! (*She forces a laugh*) I suppose all this

70

sounds too preposterous. Well, maybe it was the booze working. I'd had a lot. (*She reaches for a cigarette—returning to her hard flippancy*) And then followed my little dip into adultery.

ELSA

(*With a little shiver of repulsion*)

Oh!

LUCY

But what a hideous bore this must be to you. Why did I have to tell you, I wonder. It was the last thing I ever wanted— (*Turns on her in a flash of resentful vindictiveness*) It makes me out worse than you expected, eh? But suppose John were unfaithful to you—

ELSA

(*Startled—frightenedly*)

Don't! (*Then indignantly*) Lucy! I won't have you say that, not even—

LUCY

I'm only asking you to suppose.

ELSA

I can't! I won't! And I won't let you! It's too—! (*Then controlling herself—forcing a smile*) But I'm a bigger fool than you are to get angry. You simply don't know John, that's all. You don't know what an old-fashioned romantic idealist he is at heart about love and marriage. And I thank God he is! You'll laugh at me but I know he never had a single affair in his life before he met me.

71

LUCY

Oh, come on, Elsa. That's too much!

ELSA

Oh, please don't think I'm a naïve fool. I was as cynical about men in those days as you are now. I wouldn't have believed it of another man in the world, but with John I felt it was absolutely true to what I knew he was like inside him.

LUCY

You loved him and you wanted to believe.

ELSA

No. Even before I loved him, I felt that. It was what made me love him, more than anything else—the feeling that he would be mine, only mine, that I wouldn't have to share him even with the past. If you only could realize how much that meant to me—especially at that time, when I was still full of the disgust and hurt of my first marriage.

LUCY

Well, that's all very fine, but it's not proving to me how you can be so certain that never since then—

ELSA

(*Proudly*)

I know he loves me. I know he knows how much I love him. He knows what that would do to me. It would kill forever all my faith in life—all truth, all beauty, all love! I wouldn't want to live!

LUCY

You shouldn't let yourself be so completely at the mercy of any man—not even John.

72

ELSA

I'm not afraid. (*She smiles*) The trouble with you is, you old cynic, you can't admit that our marriage is a real ideal marriage. But it is—and that's entirely John's work, not mine.

LUCY

His work?

ELSA

Yes. When I first met him I thought I was through with marriage for good. Even after I fell in love with him, I didn't want to marry. I was afraid of marriage. I proposed quite frankly that we should simply live together and each keep entire freedom of action. (*She laughs*) Oh, I was quite ultramodern about it! And it shocked John terribly, poor dear—in spite of all his old radical ideas. I'm sure it almost disillusioned him with me for life! He sternly scorned my offer. He argued with me. How he argued—like a missionary converting a heathen! He said he loathed the ordinary marriage as much as I did, but that the ideal in back of marriage was a beautiful one, and he knew we could realize that ideal.

LUCY

Ah, yes, the ideal! I heard a little talk about that once, too!

ELSA

He said no matter if every other marriage on earth were rotten and a lie, our love could make ours into a true sacrament —sacrament was the word he used—a sacrament of faith in which each of us would find the completest self-expression in making our union a beautiful thing. (*She smiles lovingly*) You see, all this was what I had longed to hear the man I loved say

73

about the spiritual depth of his love for me—what every woman dreams of hearing her lover say, I think.

LUCY

(*Stirring uneasily—mechanically*)

Yes. I know.

ELSA

And, of course, it blew my petty modern selfishness right out the window. I couldn't believe he meant it at first, but when I saw he did, that finished me. (*She smiles—then with quiet pride*) And I think we've lived up to that ideal ever since. I hope I have. I know he has. It was his creation, you see.

LUCY

Of course he has. Of course.

ELSA

And our marriage has meant for us, not slavery or boredom but freedom and harmony within ourselves—and happiness. So we must have both lived true to it. Happiness is proof, isn't it?

LUCY

(*Deeply moved—without looking at* ELSA, *takes her hand and squeezes it—huskily*)

Of course it is. Please forget the stupid rot I've said. I was only trying to get a rise out of you. We all know how wonderfully happy you and John are. Only remember, the world is full of spiteful liars who would do anything to wreck your happiness and drag you down to their level—what I was doing. So never listen— But of course you won't, will you? You have faith. (*She turns and kisses her impulsively*) God bless you—and preserve your happiness!

ELSA

Thank you, Lucy. That's dear of you. (*Then puzzledly*) But why should you be afraid that any one—

LUCY

(*Jumps to her feet nervously*)

Only my morbidness. I've been accused of so many rotten things I never did that I suppose I'm hipped on the subject. (*Then abruptly*) Got to run now, Elsa—go home and get on my armor for another of Walter's parties. It's a gay life. The only hope is he'll be so broke before long no one will call on us but our forgotten friends. (*She gives a bitter little laugh and starts to go around the left of sofa—then, at a noise of a door opening in the hall—nervously*) Isn't that some one—?

ELSA

It must be John. (*She hurries around the right of sofa and back toward the doorway.*)

JOHN

(*Calls from the hall*)

Hello.

ELSA

(*Going out, meets him as he appears in the hall just beyond the doorway—kissing him*)

Hello, darling. You're early. I'm so glad.

JOHN

I thought, as I'd told Uncle to come early, I better— (*He kisses her*) How do you feel, dear? You look much better.

ELSA

Oh, I'm fine, John. (LUCY *has remained standing by the left corner of the sofa, in a stiff, strained attitude, the expression on her face that of one caught in a corner, steeling herself for an ordeal.* ELSA *and* JOHN *come in, their arms around each other. As they do so,* LUCY *recovers her poise and calls to him*)

LUCY

Hello, John.

JOHN

(*Coming to her, his face wearing its most cordial, poker-faced smile*)

Why, hello, Lucy. I thought I heard a familiar voice when I came in. (*They shake hands*) A pleasant surprise. Been a long time since we've had this pleasure. (ELSA *has come forward behind him. The figure of the masked* LOVING *appears in the doorway. During the next few speeches he moves silently to the corner of the long table before the window, right-front, and stands there, without looking at them, facing front, his eyes fixed in the same cold stare, the expression of his masked face seeming to be more than ever sneering and sinister.*)

LUCY

Now, don't you begin on that! Elsa has already given me hell.

ELSA

(*Laughing*)

And she's repented and been forgiven.

JOHN

Oh, that's all right, then.

LUCY
(*Nervously*)
I was just leaving. Sorry I've got to run, John.

ELSA
Oh, you can't, now. John will think he's driven you out.

LUCY
No, really, Elsa, I—

ELSA
You simply must keep John company for a few minutes. Because I've got to go to the kitchen. I trust Emmy on ordinary occasions, but when a long-lost uncle is coming to dinner, a little personal supervision is in order. (*She moves toward the dining-room at left.*)

LUCY
(*With a note of desperation*)
Well—but I can't stay more than a second.

ELSA
I'll be back right away. (*She disappears through the dining-room door. The moment she is gone,* JOHN's *cordial smile vanishes and his face takes on a tense, harried look. He is now standing behind the right end of sofa,* LUCY *behind the left end. In the pause while they wait for* ELSA *to get out of earshot,* LOVING *moves silently over until he is standing just behind* JOHN *but a step toward rear from him, facing half toward him, half toward front.*)

JOHN
(*Lowering his voice—hurriedly*)
I hope you've been careful and not said anything that—

LUCY

Might give you away? Of course, I didn't. And even if I were rotten enough to come right out and tell her, she'd never believe me, she has such a touching faith in you.

JOHN

(*Wincing*)

Don't!

LUCY

No. You're perfectly safe. There's only one thing I've got to warn you about. It's nothing, really, but—

JOHN

What?

LUCY

Walter has been telling people. He has to, you see, to keep up his pose of friendly understanding—

JOHN

But how does Walter know?

LUCY

Don't look so dismayed! He doesn't know—who it was. And you'd be the last one he'd ever suspect.

JOHN

How is it he knows about you?

LUCY

(*Hesitates—then defiantly*)

I told him.

78

JOHN

You told him? In God's name, why? But I know. You couldn't resist—watching him squirm!

LUCY

(*Stung*)

Exactly, John. Why do you suppose I ever did it, except for his benefit—if you want the truth.

JOHN

Good God, don't you think I know that? Do you imagine I ever thought it was anything but revenge on your part?

LUCY

And whom were you revenging yourself on, John?—now we're being frank.

LOVING

(*With sinister mockery*)

Who knows? Perhaps on love. Perhaps, in my soul, I hate love!

LUCY

(*Stares at* JOHN *with frightened bewilderment*)

John! Now you're like—that night!

JOHN

(*Confusedly*)

I? It wasn't I. (*Angrily*) What do you mean by saying I was revenging myself? Why should I revenge myself on her?

LUCY

I don't know, John. That's a matter for your conscience. I've got enough on my own, thank you. I must say I resent your attitude, John. (*With a flippant sneer*) Hardly the lover-like tone, is it?

JOHN

(*With disgust*)

Lover!

LUCY

Oh, I know. I feel the same way. But why hate me? Why not hate yourself?

JOHN

As if I didn't! Good God, if you knew! (*Then bitterly*) And how long do you think you'll be able to resist telling Walter it was I, his old friend—so you can watch him squirm some more!

LUCY

John!

JOHN

And Walter will have to tell that to every one, too—to live up to his pose! And then—

LUCY

John! You know I wouldn't, even if I hated you as you seem to hate me. I wouldn't for Elsa's sake. Oh, I know you think I'm a rotten liar, but I love Elsa! (*Then brokenly*) Oh, it's such a vile mess! What fools we were!

JOHN

(*Dully*)

Yes. (*Bitterly again*) I'm sorry I can't trust you, Lucy. I can when you're yourself. But full of booze— I see what it

will come to. I'll have to tell her myself to save her the humiliation of hearing it through dirty gossip!

LUCY

John! Oh, please don't be such a fool! Please!

JOHN

You think she couldn't forgive?

LUCY

I'm thinking of what it would do to her. Can't you see—?

JOHN

(*Warningly, as he hears the pantry door opening*)
Ssshh! (*Quickly, raising his voice to a conversational tone*)
Uncle is a grand old fellow. You'll have to meet him some
time. You'd like him.

LUCY

I'm sure I would. (*Then, as* ELSA *comes in from the dining-
room*) Ah, here you are. Well, I've got to fly. (*She holds out
her hand to* JOHN) Good-bye, John. Take care of Elsa.

JOHN

Good-bye, Lucy. (ELSA *puts an arm around her waist and
they go back to the hall doorway.*)

ELSA

I'll get your things.
(*They disappear in the hall. As soon as they have gone,*
JOHN *turns and, coming around the sofa, sits down on
it and stares before him with hunted eyes.* LOVING *moves*

until he is standing directly behind him. He bends over and whispers mockingly.)

LOVING

I warned you it was closing in! You had better make up your mind now to tell the rest of your novel to-night—while there is still time!

JOHN
(*Tensely*)

Yes. I must.

LOVING

But, first, it still remains to decide what is to be your hero's end. (*He gives a little jeering laugh*) Strange, isn't it, what difficult problems your little dabble in fiction has brought up which demand a final answer! (*He laughs again—then turns to face the doorway as* ELSA *reënters the room. His eyes remain fixed on her as she comes forward. She comes quietly to the right end of the sofa.* JOHN *does not notice her coming.* LOVING *remains standing at right, rear, of* JOHN.)

ELSA

A penny for your thoughts, John. (*He starts. She sits down beside him—with a smile*) Did I scare you?

JOHN
(*Forcing a smile*)

Don't know what's the matter with me. I seem to have the nervous jumps lately. (*Then carelessly*) Glad to see Lucy again, were you?

ELSA

Yes—of course. Only she's changed so. Poor Lucy.

JOHN

Why poor? Oh, you mean on account of Walter's antics?

ELSA

Then you know?

JOHN

Who doesn't? He's been making as public an ass of himself
as possible. But let's not talk about Walter. What did you think
of the big event to-day: Uncle dropping out of the blue?

ELSA

It must have been a surprise for you. I'm dying to meet him.
I'm so glad he could come to-night.

JOHN

Yes. So am I. (*As if his conversation had run dry, he falls
into an uneasy silence.* ELSA *looks at him worriedly. Then she
nestles up close to him.*)

ELSA

(*Tenderly*)

Still love me, do you?

JOHN

(*Takes her in his arms and kisses her—with intense feeling*)

You know I do! There's nothing in life I give a damn about
except your love! You know that, don't you?

ELSA

Yes, dear.

JOHN

(*Avoiding her eyes now*)

And you'll always love me—no matter what an unworthy
fool I am?

ELSA

Ssshh! You mustn't say things like that. It's not true. (*Then smiling teasingly*) Well, if you love me so much, prove it by telling me.

JOHN
(*Controlling a start*)

Telling you what?

ELSA

Now, don't pretend. I know there's something that's been troubling you for weeks—ever since I came back from Boston.

JOHN

No, honestly, Elsa.

ELSA

Something you're keeping back because you're afraid of worrying me. So you might as well confess.

JOHN
(*Forcing a smile*)

Confess? And will you promise—to forgive?

ELSA

Forgive you for not wanting to worry me? Foolish one!

JOHN
(*Hurriedly*)

No, I was only joking. There's nothing.

ELSA

Now! But I think I can guess. It's about business, isn't it?

JOHN
(*Grasps at this*)

Well—yes, if you must know.

ELSA

And you were afraid that would upset me? Oh, John, you're such a child at times you ought to be spanked. You must think I've become a poor, helpless doll!

JOHN

No, but—

ELSA

Just because you've pampered me so terribly the past few years! But remember, we had barely enough to get along on when we were married—and I didn't appear so terribly unhappy then, did I? And no matter how poor we become, do you think it would ever really matter one bit to me as long as I had you?

JOHN

(*Stammers miserably*)

Sweetheart! You make me feel—so damned ashamed! God, I can't tell you!

ELSA

(*Kissing him*)

But, darling, it's nothing! And now promise me you'll forget it and not worry any more?

JOHN

Yes.

ELSA

Good! Let's talk of something else. Tell me, have you been doing anything more on the rest of your idea for a novel?

JOHN

Yes, I— I've got most of it thought out.

85

ELSA

(*Encouragingly*)

That's splendid. You just put your mind on that and forget your silly worries. But when am I going to hear it?

JOHN

Well, I told Uncle the first part and he was curious, too. So I threatened him I might give you both an outline of the rest to-night.

ELSA

Oh, that's fine. (*Then she laughs*) And I'll confess it will be a great aid to me as a hostess. I'll probably feel a bit self-conscious, entertaining a strange priest-uncle for the first time.

JOHN

Oh, you won't be with him a minute before you'll feel he's an old friend.

ELSA

Well, that sounds encouraging. But you tell your story just the same. (*She gets up*) It must be getting on. I'd better go up and start getting dressed. (*She goes around the left end of the sofa and back toward the hall door*) Are you going up to your study for a while?

JOHN

Yes, in a minute. I want to do a little more work on my plot. The end isn't clearly worked out yet.

LOVING

That is, my hero's end!

86

DAYS WITHOUT END

ELSA

(*Smiling at* JOHN *encouragingly*)

Then you get busy, by all means, so you'll have no excuse!

(*She goes out. As soon as she is gone,* JOHN's *expression changes and becomes tense and hunted again.* LOVING *remains standing behind him, staring down at him with cold, scornful eyes. There is a pause of silence.*)

JOHN

(*Suddenly—his face full of the bitterest, tortured self-loathing —aloud to himself*)

You God-damned rotten swine!

LOVING

(*Mockingly*)

Yes, unfit to live. Quite unfit for life, I think. But there is always death to wash one's sins away—sleep, untroubled by Love's betraying dream! (*He gives a low, sinister laugh*) Merely a consoling reminder—in case you've forgotten! (JOHN *listens fascinatedly, as if to an inner voice. Then a look of terror comes into his face and he shudders.*)

JOHN

(*Torturedly*)

For God's sake! Leave me alone!

Curtain

ACT THREE

PLOT FOR A NOVEL

(*Continued*)

ACT THREE

Scene I

SCENE—*The living-room again. It is immediately after dinner.* FATHER BAIRD *is sitting in the chair at left, front,* ELSA *on the sofa,* JOHN *beside her on her left, the masked* LOVING *at right, rear, of* JOHN, *in the chair by the end of the table before the window.* JOHN *and* LOVING *are in dinner clothes of identical cut.* ELSA *wears a white evening gown of extremely simple lines.* FATHER BAIRD *is the same as in Act One.*

MARGARET *is serving them the after-dinner coffee. She goes out through the dining-room door.*

JOHN
(*Puts an arm around* ELSA's *waist playfully*)
Well, now you've got to know her, what do you think of her, Uncle? Weren't my letters right?

FATHER BAIRD
(*Gallantly*)
They were much too feeble. You didn't do her justice by half!

ELSA
Thank you, Father. It's so kind of you to say that.

JOHN

Ah! I told you that was one subject we'd agree on! (*Then to* ELSA *in a tenderly chiding tone*) But I've got a bone to pick with you, my lady. You ate hardly any dinner, do you know it?

ELSA

Oh, but I did, dear.

JOHN

No, you only went through the motions. I was watching you. That's no way to get back your strength.

FATHER BAIRD

Yes, you need all the nourishment you can take when you're getting over the flu.

JOHN

(*Worriedly—grasping her hand*)

Sure you're warm enough? Want me to get you something to put over your shoulders?

ELSA

No, dear, thank you.

JOHN

Remember it's a rotten, chilly, rainy day out and even indoors you can't be too careful.

ELSA

Oh, but I'm quite all right now, John. Please don't worry about me.

JOHN

Well, don't let yourself get tired now, you hear? If you find yourself feeling at all worn-out, you just send Uncle and me off to my study. He'll understand. Won't you, Uncle?

FATHER BAIRD

Of course. I hope Elsa will feel I'm one of the family and treat me without ceremony.

ELSA

I do feel that, Father. (*Then teasingly*) But do you know what I think is behind all this solicitude of John's? He's simply looking for an excuse to get out of telling us the rest of his novel. But we won't let him back out, will we?

FATHER BAIRD

Indeed we won't.

ELSA

The first part is so unusual and interesting. Don't you think so, Father?

FATHER BAIRD

(*Quietly*)

Yes. Tragic and revealing to me.

ELSA

You see, John, it's no use. We're simply going to insist.

LOVING

(*Coldly mocking*)

You're sure—you insist?

ELSA

Of course I do. So come on.

JOHN

(*Nervously*)

Well— (*He hesitates—gulps down the rest of his coffee.*)

ELSA

(*Smiling*)

I never saw you so flustered before, John. You'd think you were going to address an audience of literary critics.

JOHN

(*Begins jerkily*)

Well— But before I start, there's one thing I want to impress on you both again. My plot, up to the last part, which is wholly imaginary, is taken from life. It's the story of a man I once knew.

LOVING

(*Mockingly*)

Or thought I knew.

ELSA

May I be inquisitive? Did I ever know the man?

LOVING

(*A hostile, repellent note in his voice*)

No. I can swear to that. You have never known him.

ELSA

(*Taken aback, gives* JOHN *a wondering look—then apologetically*)

I'm sorry I butted in with a silly question. Go on, dear.

DAYS WITHOUT END

JOHN

(*Nervously—forcing a laugh*)

I— It's hard getting started. (*He turns and reaches for his coffee, forgetting he has drunk it—sets the cup down again abruptly and goes on hurriedly*) Well, you will remember my first part ended when the boy's parents had died.

LOVING

And he had denied all his old superstitions!

JOHN

Well, as you can imagine, for a long while after their deaths, he went through a terrific inner conflict. He was seized by fits of terror, in which he felt he really had given his soul to some evil power. He would feel a tortured longing to pray and beg for forgiveness. It seemed to him that he had forsworn all love forever—and was cursed. At these times he wanted only to die. Once he even took his father's revolver—

LOVING

(*Sneeringly*)

But he was afraid to face death. He was still too religious-minded, you see, to accept the one beautiful, comforting truth of life: that death is final release, the warm, dark peace of annihilation.

FATHER BAIRD

(*Quietly*)

I cannot see the beauty and comfort.

LOVING

He often regretted afterwards he had not had the courage to die then. It would have saved him so much silly romantic pursuit of meaningless illusions.

95

ELSA

(*Uneasily*)

Oh, you mustn't talk that way, John. It sounds so bitter—and false—coming from you.

JOHN

(*Confusedly*)

I— I didn't— You forget I'm simply following what this man told me. (*Hurrying on*) Well, finally, he came out of this period of black despair. He taught himself to take a rationalistic attitude. He read all sorts of scientific books. He ended up by becoming an atheist. But his experience had left an indelible scar on his spirit. There always remained something in him that felt itself damned by life, damned with distrust, cursed with the inability ever to reach a lasting belief in any faith, damned by a fear of the lie hiding behind the mask of truth.

FATHER BAIRD

Ah!

LOVING

(*Sneeringly*)

So romantic, you see—to think of himself as possessed by a damned soul!

JOHN

And in after years, even at the height of his rationalism, he never could explain away a horror of death—and a strange fascination it had for him. And coupled with this was a dread of life—as if he constantly sensed a malignant Spirit hiding behind life, waiting to catch men at its mercy, in their hour of secure happiness— Something that hated life!— Something that laughed with mocking scorn! (*He stares before him with a fascinated dread, as if he saw this Something before him. Then, suddenly, as if in reply,* LOVING *gives a little mocking laugh, barely audible.* JOHN *shudders.* ELSA *and* FATHER BAIRD *start and stare at* JOHN *uneasily, but he is looking straight ahead and they turn away again.*)

LOVING

A credulous, religious-minded fool, as I've pointed out! And he carried his credulity into the next period of his life, where he believed in one social or philosophical Ism after another, always on the trail of Truth! He was never courageous enough to face what he really knew was true, that there is no truth for men, that human life is unimportant and meaningless. No. He was always grasping at some absurd new faith to find an excuse for going on!

JOHN

(*Proudly*)

And he did go on! And he found his truth at last—in love, where he least expected he ever would find it. For he had always been afraid of love. And when he met the woman who afterwards became his wife and realized he was in love with her, it threw him into a panic of fear. He wanted to run away from her—but found he couldn't.

LOVING

(*Scornfully*)

So he weakly surrendered—and immediately began building a new superstition of love around her.

97

JOHN

He was happy again for the first time since his parents' death—to his bewildered joy.

LOVING

(*Mockingly*)

And secret fear!

ELSA

(*Gives* JOHN *a curious, uneasy glance*)

Secret fear?

JOHN

Yes, he—he came to be afraid of his happiness. His love made him feel at the mercy of that mocking Something he dreaded. And the more peace and security he found in his wife's love, the more he was haunted by fits of horrible foreboding—the recurrent dread that she might die and he would be left alone again, without love. So great was the force of this obsession at times that he felt caught in a trap, desperate—

LOVING

And he often found himself regretting—

JOHN

(*Hastily*)

Against his will—

LOVING

(*Inexorably*)

That he had again let love put him at the mercy of life!

JOHN

(*Hurriedly*)

But, of course, he realized this was all morbid and ridiculous—for wasn't he happier than he had ever dreamed he could be again?

LOVING
(With gloating mockery)
And so he deliberately destroyed that happiness!

ELSA
(Startledly)
Destroyed his happiness? How, John?

JOHN
(Turns to her, forcing a smile)
I'm afraid you will find this part of his story hard to believe, Elsa. This damned fool, who loved his wife more than anything else in life, was unfaithful to her. (FATHER BAIRD *starts and stares at him with a shocked expression.*)

ELSA
(Frightenedly)
It is—hard to believe. But this part is all the story of the man you knew, isn't it?

JOHN
Yes, of course, and you mustn't condemn him entirely until you've heard how it came to happen. (*He turns away from her again—jerkily*) His wife had gone away. It was the first time. He felt lost without her—fearful, disintegrated. His familiar dread seized him. He began imagining all sorts of catastrophes. Horrible pictures formed in his mind. She was run over by a car. Or she had caught pneumonia and lay dying. Every day these evil visions possessed him. He tried

to escape them in work. He couldn't. (*He pauses for a second, nerving himself to go on. Then starts again*) Then one night an old friend called—to drag him off to a party. He loathed such affairs usually, but this time he thought it would help him to escape himself for a while. So he went. He observed with disgust how his friend, who was drunk, was pawing over some woman right under the nose of his wife. He knew that this friend was continually having affairs of this sort and that his wife was aware of it. He had often wondered if she cared, and he was curious now to watch her reactions. And very soon he had an example of what her pride had to endure, for the husband went off openly with his lady. The man felt a great sympathy for her—and, as if she guessed his thought, she came to him, and he overdid himself in being kind. (*He gives a short bitter laugh*) A great mistake! For she reacted to it in a way that at first shocked him but ended up in arousing his curiosity. He had known her for years. It wasn't like her. It fascinated him, in a way, that she should have become so corrupted. He became interested to see how far she would go with it—purely as an observer, he thought— the poor idiot! (*He laughs again.* FATHER BAIRD *has remained motionless, his eyes on the floor.* ELSA'S *face is pale and set, her eyes have a bewildered, stricken look.* JOHN *goes on*) Remember, all this time he saw through her; he laughed to himself at her crude vamping; he felt he was only playing a game. Just as he knew she was playing a game; that it was no desire for him but hatred for her husband that inspired her. (*He gives a short contemptuous laugh again*) Oh, he had it all analyzed quite correctly, considering the known elements. It was the unknown—

FATHER BAIRD

(*Without raising his head*)

Yes. (*He casts a quick glance at* ELSA, *then looks as quickly away. Her eyes are fastened on the floor now. Her face has frozen into a mask with the tense effort she is making not to give herself away.*)

JOHN

He had not the slightest desire for this woman. When she threw herself into his arms, he was repelled. He determined to end the game. He thought of his wife— (*He forces a laugh*) But, as I've said, there was the unknown to reckon with. At the thought of his wife, suddenly it was as if something outside him, a hidden spirit of evil, took possession of him.

LOVING

(*Coldly vindictive now*)

That is, he saw clearly that this situation was the climax of a long death struggle between his wife and him. The woman with him counted only as a means. He saw that underneath all his hypocritical pretenses he really hated love. He wanted to deliver himself from its power and be free again. He wanted to kill it!

ELSA

(*With horrified pain*)

Oh! (*Trying to control herself*) I—I don't understand. He hated love? He wanted to kill it? But that's—too horrible!

JOHN

(*Stammers confusedly*)

No—I— Don't you see it wasn't he?

LOVING

But, I'm afraid, Elsa, that my hero's silly idea that he was possessed by a demon must strike you as an incredible superstitious excuse to lie out of his responsibility.

FATHER BAIRD

(*Without lifting his eyes—quietly*)

Quite credible to me, Jack. One may not give one's soul to a devil of hate—and remain forever scatheless.

LOVING

(*Sneeringly*)

As for the adultery itself, the truth is that this poor fool was making a great fuss about nothing—an act as meaningless as that of one fly with another, of equal importance to life!

ELSA

(*Stares at* JOHN *as if he had become a stranger—a look of sick repulsion coming over her face*)

John! You're disgusting! (*She shrinks away from him to the end of the sofa near* FATHER BAIRD.)

JOHN

(*Stammers confusedly*)

But I—I didn't mean—forgive me. I only said that—as a joke —to get a rise out of Uncle.

FATHER BAIRD

(*Gives a quick anxious look at* ELSA—*then quietly, an undercurrent of sternness in his voice*)

I don't think it's a joke. But go on with your story, Jack.

102

JOHN

(*Forcing himself to go on*)

Well I—I know you can imagine the hell he went through from the moment he came to himself and realized the vileness he had been guilty of. He couldn't forgive himself—and that's what his whole being now cried out for—forgiveness!

FATHER BAIRD

(*Quietly*)

I can well believe that, Jack.

JOHN

He wanted to tell his wife and beg for forgiveness—but he was afraid of losing her love. (*He gives a quick glance at* ELSA, *as if to catch her reaction to this, but she is staring straight before her with a still, set face. He forces a smile and adopts a joking tone*) And here's where I'd like to have your opinion, Elsa. The question doesn't come up in my story, as you'll see, but— Could his wife have forgiven him, do you think?

ELSA

(*Starts—then tensely*)

You want me to put myself in the wife's place?

JOHN

Yes. I want to see whether the man was a fool or not—in his fear.

ELSA

(*After a second's pause—tensely*)

No. She could never forgive him.

JOHN

(*Desperately*)

But it wasn't he! Can't you see—

ELSA

No. I'm afraid—I can't see.

JOHN

(*Dully now*)

Yes. That's what I thought you'd say.

ELSA

But what does it matter what I think? You said the question of her forgiving doesn't come up in your novel.

LOVING

(*Coldly*)

Not while the wife is alive.

JOHN

(*Dully*)

He never tells her.

LOVING

She becomes seriously ill.

ELSA

(*With a start*)

Oh.

LOVING

(*In a cold voice, as if he were pronouncing a death sentence*)

Flu, which turns into pneumonia. And she dies.

ELSA

(Frightenedly now)

Dies?

LOVING

Yes. I need her death for my end. *(Then in a sinister, jeering tone)* That is, to make my romantic hero come finally to a rational conclusion about his life!

ELSA

(Stares before her, not seeming to have heard this last—her eyes full of a strange, horrified fascination—as if she were talking aloud to herself)

So she dies.

FATHER BAIRD

(After a worried glance at her—an undercurrent of warning in his quiet tone)

I think you've tired Elsa out with your sensational imaginings, Jack. I'd spare her, for the present, at least, the fog of gloom your novel is plunging into.

ELSA

(Grasps at this—tensely)

Yes, I'm afraid it has been too exciting— I really don't feel up to— During dinner I began to get a headache and it's splitting now.

JOHN

(Gets up—worriedly)

But why didn't you tell me? If I'd known that, I'd never have bored you with my damned plot.

ELSA

I—I think I'll lie down here on the sofa—and take some aspirin—and rest for a while. You can go with your uncle up to your study—and tell him the rest of your story there.

FATHER BAIRD

(*Gets up*)

An excellent idea. Come on, Jack, and give your poor wife a respite from the horrors of authorship. (*He goes to the doorway in rear.*)

JOHN

(*Comes to* ELSA. *As he does so,* LOVING *comes and stands behind her, at rear of sofa*)

I'm so darned sorry, Elsa, if I've—

ELSA

Oh, please! It's only a headache.

JOHN

You—you don't feel really sick, do you, dearest? (*He puts a hand to her forehead timidly.*)

ELSA

(*Shrinks from his touch*)

No, no, it's nothing.

LOVING

(*Slowly, in his cold tone with its undercurrent of sinister hidden meaning*)

You must be very careful, Elsa. Remember it's cold and raining out.

DAYS WITHOUT END

ELSA

(*Staring before her strangely—repeats fascinatedly*)
It's raining?

LOVING

Yes.

JOHN

(*Stammers confusedly*)
Yes, you—you must be careful, dearest.

FATHER BAIRD

(*From the doorway in rear—sharply*)
Come along, Jack! (JOHN *goes back to him and* LOVING *follows* JOHN. FATHER BAIRD *goes into the hall, turning left to go upstairs to the study.* JOHN *stops in the doorway and looks back for a moment at* ELSA *frightenedly.* LOVING *comes to his side and also stops and looks at her, his eyes cold and remorseless in his mask of sinister mockery. They stand there for a moment side by side. Then* JOHN *turns and disappears in the hall toward left, following* FATHER BAIRD. LOVING *remains, his gaze concentrated on the back of* ELSA's *head with a cruel, implacable intensity. She is still staring before her with the same strange fascinated dread. Then, as if in obedience to his will, she rises slowly to her feet and walks slowly and woodenly back past him and disappears in the hall, turning right toward the entrance door to the apartment. For a second* LOVING *remains looking after her. Then he turns and disappears in the hall toward left, following* FATHER BAIRD *and* JOHN *to the study.*)

Curtain

ACT THREE

Scene II

Scene—JOHN LOVING's *study on the upper floor of the apartment. At left, front, is a door leading into* ELSA's *bedroom. Bookcases extend along the rear and right walls. There is a door to the upper hall at rear, right. A long table with a lamp is at center, front. At left of table is a chair. In front of table a similar chair. At right, front, is a chaise-longue, facing left.*

FATHER BAIRD, JOHN *and* LOVING *are discovered. The priest is sitting on the chaise-longue,* JOHN *in the chair at front of table,* LOVING *in the chair at left of table.* FATHER BAIRD *sits in the same attitude as he had in the previous scene, his eyes on the floor, his expression sad and a bit stern.* LOVING's *masked face stares at* JOHN, *his eyes cold and still.* JOHN *is talking in a strained tone, monotonously, insistently. It is as if he were determinedly talking to keep himself from thinking.*

JOHN

I listen to people talking about this universal breakdown we are in and I marvel at their stupid cowardice. It is so obvious that they deliberately cheat themselves because their fear of change won't let them face the truth. They don't want to understand what has happened to them. All they want is to start the merry-go-round of blind greed all over again. They no longer know what they want this country to be, what they want it to become, where they want it to go. It has lost all meaning for them except as a pig-wallow. And so their lives as citizens have no beginnings, no ends. They have lost the ideal of the Land of the Free. Freedom demands initiative, courage, the need to decide what life must mean to oneself. To them, that is terror. They explain away their spiritual cowardice by whining that the time for individualism is past, when it is their courage to possess their own souls which is dead—and stinking! No, they don't want to be free. Slavery means security—of a kind, the only kind they have courage for. It means they need not think. They have only to obey orders from owners who are, in turn, their slaves!

LOVING

(Breaks in—with bored scorn)

But I'm denouncing from my old soap box again. It's all silly twaddle, of course. Freedom was merely our romantic delusion. We know better now. We know we are all the slaves of meaningless chance—electricity or something, which whirls us—on to Hercules!

JOHN

(With a proud assertiveness)

But, in spite of that, I say: Very well! On to Hercules! Let us face that! Once we have accepted it without evasion, we can begin to create new goals for ourselves, ends for our days! A new discipline for life will spring into being, a new will and power to live, a new ideal to measure the value of our lives by!

LOVING

(*Mockingly*)

What? Am I drooling on about my old social ideals again? Sorry to bore you, Uncle.

FATHER BAIRD

(*Quietly, without looking up*)

You are not boring me, Jack.

JOHN

(*An idealistic exaltation coming into his voice*)

We need a new leader who will teach us that ideal, who by his life will exemplify it and make it a living truth for us—a man who will prove that man's fleeting life in time and space can be noble. We need, above all, to learn again to believe in the possibility of nobility of spirit in ourselves! A new savior must be born who will reveal to us how we can be saved from ourselves, so that we can be free of the past and inherit the future and not perish by it!

LOVING

(*Mockingly*)

Must sound like my old letters to you, Uncle. It's more nonsense, of course. But there are times of stress and flight when one hides in any old empty barrel!

FATHER BAIRD

(*Ignoring this—quietly*)

You are forgetting that men have such a Savior, Jack. All they need is to remember Him.

JOHN

(*Slowly*)

Yes, perhaps if we could again have faith in—

LOVING

(*Harshly*)

No! We have passed beyond gods! There can be no going back!

FATHER BAIRD

Jack! Take care!

LOVING

(*Mockingly again*)

But, on the other hand, I'll grant you the pseudo-Nietzschean savior I just evoked out of my past is an equally futile ghost. Even if he came, we'd only send him to the insane asylum for teaching that we should have a nobler aim for our lives than getting all four feet in a trough of swill! (*He laughs sardonically*) How could we consider such an unpatriotic idea as anything but insane, eh? (*There is a pause.* FATHER BAIRD *looks up and studies* JOHN's *face searchingly, hopefully.*)

FATHER BAIRD

(*Finally speaks quietly*)

Jack, ever since we came upstairs, I've listened patiently while you've discussed every subject under the sun except the one I know is really on your mind.

JOHN

I don't know what you mean.

III

FATHER BAIRD

The end of your story.

JOHN

Oh, forget that. I'm sick of the damned thing—now, at any rate.

FATHER BAIRD

Sick of the damned thing, yes. That's why I feel it's important you tell it—now. This man's wife dies, you said. (*He stares fixedly at* JOHN *now and adds slowly*) Of influenza which turns into pneumonia.

JOHN
(*Uneasily*)

Why do you stare like that?

FATHER BAIRD
(*Dropping his eyes—quietly*)

Go on with your story.

JOHN
(*Hesitantly*)

Well—I— You can imagine the anguish he feels after his wife's death—the guilt which tortures him a thousandfold now she is dead.

FATHER BAIRD

I can well imagine it, Jack.

LOVING
(*Sneeringly*)

And under the influence of his ridiculous guilty conscience, all the superstitions of his childhood, which he had prided himself his reason had killed, return to plague him. He feels at times an absurd impulse to pray. He fights this nonsense back. He analyzes it rationally. He sees it clearly as a throw-back to boyhood experiences. But, in spite of himself, that cowardly something in him he despises as superstition seduces his reason with the old pathetic lie of survival after death. He begins to believe his wife is alive in some mythical hereafter!

JOHN

(*Strangely*)

He knows she knows of his sin now. He can hear her promis-ing to forgive if he can only believe again in his old God of Love, and seek her through Him. She will be beside him in spirit in this life, and at his death she will be waiting. Death will not be an end but a new beginning, a reunion with her in which their love will go on forever within the eternal peace and love of God! (*His voice has taken on a note of intense longing.*)

FATHER BAIRD

Ah, then you do see, Jack! Thank God!

JOHN

(*As if he hadn't heard*)

One night when he is hounded beyond endurance he rushes out—in the hope that if he walks himself into exhaustion he may be able to sleep for a while and forget. (*Strangely, staring before him, as if he were visualizing the scene he is describing*) Without his knowing how he got there, he finds he has walked in a circle and is standing before the old church, not far from where he now lives, in which he used to pray as a boy.

LOVING

(Jeeringly)

And now we come to the great temptation scene, in which he finally confronts his ghosts! *(With harsh defiance)* The church challenges him—and he accepts the challenge and goes in!

JOHN

He finds himself kneeling at the foot of the Cross. And he feels he is forgiven, and the old comforting peace and security and joy steal back into his heart! *(He hesitates, as if reluctant to go on, as if this were the end.)*

FATHER BAIRD

(Deeply moved)

And that is your end? Thank God!

LOVING

(Jeeringly)

I'm afraid your rejoicing is a bit premature—for this cowardly giving in to his weakness is not the end! Even while he is kneeling, there is a mocking rational something in him that laughs with scorn—and at the last moment his will and pride revive in him again! He sees clearly by the light of reason the degradation of his pitiable surrender to old ghostly comforts—and he rejects them! *(His voice with surprising suddenness takes on a savage vindictive quality)* He curses his God again as he had when a boy! He defies Him finally! He—!

FATHER BAIRD
(Sternly)

Jack! Take care!

JOHN
(Protests confusedly)

No—that's not right—I—

LOVING
(Strangely confused in his turn—hurriedly)

Pardon me, Uncle. Of course, that's wrong—afraid for a moment I let an author's craving for a dramatic moment run away with my sane judgment. Naturally, he could never be so stupid as to curse what he knew didn't exist!

JOHN
(Despondently)

No. He realizes he can never believe in his lost faith again. He walks out of the church—without love forever now—but daring to face his eternal loss and hopelessness, to accept it as his fate and go on with life.

LOVING
(Mockingly)

A very, very heroic end, as you see! But, unfortunately, absolutely meaningless!

FATHER BAIRD

Yes. Meaningless. I'm glad you see that.

JOHN
(Rousing a bit—defensively)

No—I take that back—it isn't meaningless. It is man's duty to life to go on!

LOVING

(Jeeringly)

The romantic idealist again speaks! On to Hercules! What an inspiring slogan! (*Then a sinister note coming into his voice*) But there is still another end to my story—the one sensible happy end!

FATHER BAIRD

(*As if he hadn't heard this last*)

Jack! Are you so blind you cannot see what your imagining his finding peace in the church reveals about the longing of your own soul—the salvation from yourself it holds out to you? Why, if you had any honesty with yourself, you would get down on your knees now and—

LOVING

Rot! How can you believe such childish superstition!

FATHER BAIRD

(*Angrily*)

Jack! I've endured all I can of your blasphemous insults to—

JOHN

(*Confused—hurriedly*)

I—I didn't mean—I'm sorry, Uncle. But it's only a story. Don't take it so seriously.

FATHER BAIRD

(*Has immediately controlled himself—quietly*)

Only a story, Jack? You're sure you still want me to believe that?

JOHN
(*Defensively*)

Why, what else could you believe? Do you think I—? (*Then in an abrupt, angry tone*) But that's enough about the damned story. I don't want to talk any more about it! (FATHER BAIRD *stares at him but keeps silent.* JOHN *starts to pace up and down with nervous restlessness—then stops abruptly*) I—if you'll excuse me—I think I'll go down and see how Elsa is. (*He goes back toward the door.* LOVING *follows him*) I'll be right back.

FATHER BAIRD
(*Quietly*)

Of course, Jack. Don't bother about me. I'll take a look at your library. (*He gets up.* JOHN *goes out.* LOVING *turns for a moment to* FATHER BAIRD, *his eyes full of a mocking derision. Then he turns and follows* JOHN. FATHER BAIRD *goes to the bookcase at right and runs his eyes over the titles of books. But he only does this mechanically. His mind is preoccupied, his expression sad and troubled.* JOHN's *voice can be heard from below calling* "Elsa." FATHER BAIRD *starts and listens. Then from* ELSA's *bedroom* JOHN's *voice is heard, as he looks for her there. He calls anxiously* "Elsa"— *then evidently hurries out again, closing the door behind him.* FATHER BAIRD's *face grows more worried. He goes to the doorway in rear and stands listening to a brief conversation from below. A moment later* JOHN *comes in from rear. He is making a great effort to conceal a feeling of dread. He comes forward.* LOVING *follows silently but stops and remains standing by the bookcase at left of doorway.*)

JOHN

She's—gone out.

FATHER BAIRD

Gone out? But it's still raining, isn't it?

JOHN

Pouring. I—I can't understand. It's a crazy thing for her to do when she's just getting over—

FATHER BAIRD
(*With an involuntary start*)

Ah!

JOHN

What?

FATHER BAIRD

Nothing.

JOHN
(*Frightenedly*)

I can't imagine—

FATHER BAIRD

How long has she been gone?

JOHN

I don't know. Margaret says she heard some one go out right after we came upstairs.

FATHER BAIRD
(*With lowered voice to himself*)

My fault, God forgive me. I had a feeling then I shouldn't leave her.

 (JOHN *sinks down in the chair by the table and waits tensely—then suddenly he bursts out*)

118

JOHN

I never should have told her the story! I'm a God-damned fool.

FATHER BAIRD

(Sternly)

You would be more honest with yourself if you said a self-damned fool! (*Hearing a sound from below*) There. Isn't that some one now? (JOHN *stops for a second to listen, then hurries to the door in rear.* LOVING *remains where he is, standing motionlessly by the bookcase.*)

JOHN

(Calls)

Is that you, Elsa?

ELSA

(From downstairs—hurriedly)

Yes. Don't come down. I'm coming up.

(*A moment later she appears in the hallway.*)

JOHN

Darling! I've been so damned worried. (*He starts to take her in his arms.*)

ELSA

Please! (*She wards him off and steps past him into the study. She has taken off her coat and hat downstairs, but the lower part of her skirt and her stockings and shoes are soaking wet. Her face is pinched and drawn and pale, with flushed spots over the cheek bones, and her eyes are bright and hard.* FATHER BAIRD *stares at her searchingly, his face sad and pitying.*)

FATHER BAIRD

(*Forcing a light tone—as she comes forward*)

Well! You have given us a scare, my lady.

ELSA

(*Tensely*)

I'm sorry, Father.

FATHER BAIRD

Your husband was half out of his mind worrying what had happened to you. (*She sits in the chair in front of table.* JOHN *stands at right of her.* LOVING *has come up and stands by the right end of table, at right, rear, of* JOHN. *His eyes are fixed on* ELSA'S *face with an eager, sinister intentness.*)

JOHN

(*With increasing uneasiness*)

Elsa! You look sick. Do you feel—?

FATHER BAIRD

I'll get her some whisky. And you make her go to bed at once. (*He goes out the door in rear.*)

JOHN

(*Grabbing her hands*)

Your hands are like ice!

ELSA

(*Pulls them away from him—coldly, without looking at him*)

It's chilly out.

JOHN

Look at your shoes! They're soaked!

120

DAYS WITHOUT END

ELSA

It doesn't matter, does it? (*A chill runs through her body.*)

JOHN

You've taken a chill. (*Then forcing a tenderly bullying tone*) You'll go right to bed, that's what. And no nonsense about it, you hear!

ELSA

Are you trying the bossy tender husband on me, John? I'm afraid that's no longer effective.

JOHN
(*Guiltily*)

Why do you say that?

ELSA

Are you determined to act out this farce to the end?

JOHN

I—I don't know what you mean. What makes you look at me—as if you hated me?

ELSA
(*Bitterly*)

Hate you? No, I only hate myself for having been such a fool! (*Then with a hard, mocking tone*) Shall I tell you where I went, and why? But perhaps I'd better put it in the form of a novel plot!

JOHN

I—I don't know what you're driving at.

ELSA

I went out because I thought I'd like to drop in on one of Lucy's parties. But it wasn't exciting—hardly any adultery going on— I had no opportunity—even if I'd been seized by any peculiar impulse of hatred and revenge on you. So I came home. (*She forces a hard, bitter laugh*) There! Are you satisfied? It's all a lie, of course. I simply went for a walk. But so is your story about the novel a lie.

JOHN
(*Stunned—stammers*)

Elsa, I—

ELSA

For God's sake, John, don't lie to me any more or I— I know, I tell you! Lucy told me all about it this afternoon.

JOHN

She told you? The damned—

ELSA

Oh, she didn't tell me it was you. But she gave me all the sordid details and they were the same as those in your story. So it was you who told on yourself. Rather a joke on you, isn't it? (*She laughs bitterly.*)

JOHN

I— (*He blurts out miserably*) Yes—it's true.

ELSA

And it was a fine joke on me, her coming here. You would appreciate it, if you had seen how I sympathized with her, how I excused her to myself and pitied her. And all the while, she

122

was pitying me! She was gloating! She's always envied us our happiness. Our happiness!

JOHN
(*Writhing*)

Don't!

ELSA

She must have been laughing at me for a fool, sneering to herself about my stupid faith in you. And you gave her that chance—you! You made our love a smutty joke for her and every one like her—you whom I loved so! And all the time I was loving you, you were only waiting for this chance to kill that love, you were hating me underneath, hating our happiness, hating the ideal of our marriage you had given me, which had become all the beauty and truth of life to me! (*She springs to her feet—distractedly*) Oh, I can't— I can't! (*She starts as if to run from the room.*)

JOHN
(*Grabbing her—imploringly*)

Elsa! For God's sake! Didn't my story explain? Can't you believe—it wasn't I? Can't you forgive?

ELSA

No! I can't forgive! How can I forgive—when all that time I loved you so, you were wishing in your heart that I would die!

JOHN
(*Frantically*)

Don't say that! It's mad! Elsa! Good God, how can you think—

123

ELSA

What else can I think? (*Then wildly*) Oh, John, stop talking! What's the good of talk? I only know I hate life! It's dirty
and insulting—and evil! I want my dream back—or I want
to be dead with it! (*She is shaken again by a wave of uncon-
trollable chill, her teeth chatter—pitiably*) Oh, John, leave me
alone! I'm cold, I'm sick. I feel crazy!

FATHER BAIRD

(*Comes in through the doorway at rear—sharply*)
Jack! Why haven't you got her to bed? Can't you see she's
ill? Phone for your doctor. (JOHN *goes out.* LOVING, *his eyes
remaining fixed on* ELSA *with the same strange look, backs out
of the doorway after him.*)

FATHER BAIRD

(*Coming to* ELSA—*with great compassion*)
My dear child, I can't tell you how deeply—

ELSA

(*Tensely*)
Don't! I can't bear— (*She is shaken again by a chill.*)

FATHER BAIRD

(*Worriedly, but trying to pretend to treat it lightly, reassur-
ingly*)
You've taken a bad chill. You were very foolhardy to— But
a day or two in bed and you'll be fine again.

ELSA

(*Strangely serious and bitterly mocking at the same time*)
But that would spoil John's story, don't you think? That

124

would be very inconsiderate after he's worked out such a convenient end for me.

FATHER BAIRD

Elsa! For the love of God, don't tell me you took his morbid nonsense seriously! Is that why you—?

ELSA
(As if she hadn't heard him)

And when he reminded me it was raining, it all seemed to fit in so perfectly—like the will of God! (*She laughs with hysterical mockery, her eyes shining feverishly.*)

FATHER BAIRD
(Sternly—more to break her mood than because he takes her impiety seriously)

Elsa! Stop that mockery! It has no part in you!

ELSA
(Confusedly)

I'm sorry. I forgot you were— (*Then suddenly hectic again*) But I've never had any God, you see—until I met John. (*She laughs hysterically—then suddenly forces control on herself and gets shakily to her feet*) I'm sorry. I seem to be talking nonsense. My head has gone woolly. I— (*JOHN enters from the hall at rear. As he comes forward, LOVING appears in the doorway behind him.*)

JOHN
(Coming to ELSA*)*

Stillwell says for you to—

ELSA

(*Distractedly*)

No! (*Then dully*) I'll go—to my room. (*She sways weakly.*
JOHN *starts toward her.*)

JOHN

Elsa! Sweetheart!

ELSA

No! (*By an effort of will, she overcomes her weakness and
walks woodenly into her bedroom and closes the door behind
her.* JOHN *makes a movement as if to follow her.*)

FATHER BAIRD

(*Sharply*)

Leave her alone, Jack.

(JOHN *sinks down hopelessly on the chaise-longue.* LOV-
ING *stands behind him, his cold eyes fixed with a sinister
intensity on the door through which* ELSA *has just dis-
appeared.* FATHER BAIRD *makes a movement as if he were
going to follow* ELSA *into her room. Then he stops. There
is an expression of sorrowful foreboding on his face.
He bows his head with a simple dignity and begins to
pray silently.*)

LOVING

(*His eyes now on* JOHN—*with a gloating mockery*)

She seems to have taken her end in your story very seriously. Let's hope she doesn't carry that too far! You have
enough on your conscience already—without murder! You
couldn't live, I know, if—

JOHN

(Shuddering—clutches his head in both hands as if to crush out his thoughts)

For God's sake! (*His eyes turn to the priest. Then their gaze travels to a point in front of* FATHER BAIRD, *and slowly his expression changes to one of fearful, fascinated awe, as if he suddenly sensed a Presence there the priest is praying to. His lips part and words come haltingly, as if they were forced out of him, full of imploring fear*) Thou wilt not—do that to me again—wilt Thou? Thou wilt not—take love from me again?

LOVING

(Jeeringly)

Is it your old demon you are praying to for mercy? Then I hope you hear his laughter! (*Then breaking into a cold, vicious rage*) You cowardly fool! I tell you there is nothing—nothing!

JOHN

(Starts back to himself—stammers with a confused air of relief)

Yes—of course—what's the matter with me? There's nothing—nothing to fear!

Curtain

ACT FOUR

THE END OF THE END

ACT FOUR

Scene I

Scene—*The study is shown as in preceding scene, but this scene also reveals the interior of* Elsa's *bedroom at left of study.*

At right of bedroom, front, is the door between the two rooms. At rear of this door, in the middle of the wall, is a dressing table, mirror and chair. In the left wall, rear, is the door to the bathroom. Before this door is a screen. At left, front, is the bed, its head against the left wall. By the head of the bed is a small stand on which is a reading lamp with a piece of cloth thrown over it to dim its light. An upholstered chair is beside the foot of the bed. Another chair is by the head of the bed at rear. A chaise-longue is at right, front, of the room.

It is nearing daybreak of a day about a week later.

In the bedroom, Elsa *lies in the bed, her eyes closed, her face pallid and wasted.* John *sits in the chair toward the foot of the bed, front. He looks on the verge of complete mental and physical collapse. His unshaven cheeks are sunken and sallow. His eyes, bloodshot from sleeplessness, stare from black hollows with a frozen anguish at* Elsa's *face.*

Loving *stands by the back of his chair, facing front. The*

131

sinister, mocking character of his mask is accentuated now, evilly intensified.

FATHER BAIRD *is standing by the middle of the bed, at rear. His face also bears obvious traces of sleepless strain. He is conferring in whispers with* DOCTOR STILLWELL, *who is standing at his right. Both are watching* ELSA *with anxious eyes. At rear of* STILLWELL *on his right, a trained nurse is standing.*

STILLWELL *is in his early fifties, tall, with a sharp, angular face and gray hair. The* NURSE *is a plump woman in her late thirties.*

For a moment after the curtain rises the whispered pantomime between STILLWELL *and the priest continues, the* NURSE *watching and listening. Then* ELSA *stirs restlessly and moans. She speaks without opening her eyes, hardly above a whisper, in a tone of despairing bitterness.*

ELSA

John! How could you? Our dream! (*She moans.*)

JOHN
(*In anguish*)

Elsa! Forgive!

LOVING
(*In a cold, inexorable tone*)

She will never forgive.

STILLWELL
(*Frowning, makes a motion to* JOHN *to be silent*)

Ssshh! (*He whispers to* FATHER BAIRD, *his eyes on* JOHN. *The priest nods and comes around the corner of the bed toward*

132

DAYS WITHOUT END

JOHN. STILLWELL *sits in the chair by the head of the bed, rear, and feels* ELSA's *pulse. The* NURSE *moves close behind him.)*

FATHER BAIRD

(Bends over JOHN's *chair and speaks in a low cautioning voice)*

Jack. You must be quiet.

JOHN

(His eyes are on STILLWELL's *face, desperately trying to read some answer there. He calls to him frightenedly)*

Doctor! What is it? Is she—?

STILLWELL

Ssshh! *(He gives* JOHN *a furious look and motions* FATHER BAIRD *to keep him quiet.)*

FATHER BAIRD

Jack! Don't you realize you're only harming her?

JOHN

(Confusedly repentant—in a low voice)

I'm sorry. I try not to, but— I know it's crazy, but I can't help being afraid—

LOVING

That my prophecy is coming true—her end in my story.

JOHN

(With anguished appeal)

No! Elsa! Don't believe that! *(*ELSA *moans.)*

FATHER BAIRD

You see! You've disturbed her again!

(STILLWELL *gets up and, after exchanging a whispered word with the* NURSE, *who nods and takes his place by the bedside, comes quicky around the end of the bed to* JOHN.)

STILLWELL

What the devil is the matter with you? I thought you promised me if I let you stay in here you'd keep quiet.

JOHN

(*Dazedly now—suddenly overcome by a wave of drowsiness he tries in vain to fight back*)
I won't again. (*His head nods.*)

STILLWELL

(*Gives him a searching look—to* FATHER BAIRD)
We've got to get him out of here.

JOHN

(*Rousing himself—desperately fighting back his drowsiness*)
I won't sleep! God, how can I sleep when—!

STILLWELL

(*Taking one arm and signaling* FATHER BAIRD *to take the other —sharply but in a voice just above a whisper*)
Loving, come into your study. I want to talk with you about your wife's condition.

134

JOHN

(*Terrified*)

Why? What do you mean? She isn't—?

STILLWELL

(*Hastily, in a forced tone of reassurance*)

No, no, no! What put that nonsense in your head? (*He flashes a signal to the priest and they both lift* JOHN *to his feet*) Come along, that's a good fellow. (*They lead* JOHN *to the door to the study at right.* LOVING *follows them silently, moving backward, his eyes fixed with sinister gloating intentness on* ELSA's *face.* FATHER BAIRD *opens the door and they pass through,* LOVING *slipping after them.* FATHER BAIRD *closes the door. They lead* JOHN *to the chaise-longue at right, front, of study, passing in front of the table.* LOVING *keeps pace with them, passing to rear of table.*

JOHN

(*Starts to resist feebly*)

Let me go! I mustn't leave her! I'm afraid! (*They get him seated on the chaise-longue,* LOVING *taking up a position directly behind him on the other side of the chaise-longue.*) I feel there's something—

LOVING

(*With a gloating mockery*)

A demon who laughs, hiding behind the end of my story! (*He gives a sinister laugh.* FATHER BAIRD *and even* STILLWELL, *in spite of himself, are appalled by this laughter.*)

JOHN
(Starts to his feet—in anguish)

No!

FATHER BAIRD

Jack!

STILLWELL

(Recovering, angry at himself and furious with JOHN—
*seizes him by the arm and forces him down on the
chaise-longue again.)*

Stop your damned nonsense! Get a grip on yourself! I've
warned you you'd go to pieces like this if you kept on refusing
to rest or take nourishment. But that's got to stop, do you hear
me? You've got to get some sleep!

FATHER BAIRD

Yes, Jack. You must!

STILLWELL

You've been a disturbing factor from the first and I've been
a fool to stand— But I've had enough! You'll stay out of her
room—

JOHN

No!

STILLWELL

Don't you want her to get well? By God, from the way
you've been acting—

JOHN
(Wildly)

For God's sake, don't say that!

136

STILLWELL

Can't you see you're no help to her in this condition? While if you'll sleep for a while—

JOHN

No! (*Imploringly*) She's much better, isn't she? For God's sake, tell me you know she isn't going to— Tell me that and I'll do anything you ask!

LOVING

And don't lie, please! I want the truth!

STILLWELL

(*Forcing an easy tone*)

What's all this talk? She's resting quietly. There's no question of— (*Then quickly*) And now I've satisfied you on that, lie down as you promised. (JOHN *stares at him uncertainly for a moment—then obediently lies down*) Close your eyes now. (JOHN *closes his eyes.* LOVING *stands by his head, staring down at his face.* JOHN *almost immediately drops off into a drugged half-sleep, his breathing becomes heavy and exhausted.* STILL- WELL *nods to* FATHER BAIRD *with satisfaction—then moves quietly to the other side of the room, by the door to* ELSA's *bed- room, beckoning* FATHER BAIRD *to follow him. He speaks to him in a low voice*) We'll have to keep an eye on him. He's headed straight for a complete collapse. But I think he'll sleep now, for a while, anyway. (*He opens the door to the bedroom, looks in and catches the eye of the* NURSE, *who is still sitting in the chair by the head of the bed, watching* ELSA. *The* NURSE *shakes her head, answering his question. He softly closes the door again.*)

FATHER BAIRD

. No change, Doctor?

STILLWELL

No. But I'm not giving up hope! She still has a fighting chance! (*Then in a tone of exasperated dejection*) If she'd only fight!

FATHER BAIRD
(*Nods with sad understanding*)

Yes. That's it.

STILLWELL

Damn it, she seems to want to die. (*Then angrily*) And, by God, in spite of his apparent grief, I've suspected at times that underneath he wants—

LOVING
(*His eyes fixed on* JOHN's *face, speaks in a cold implacable tone*)

She is going to die.

JOHN
(*Starts half-awake—mutters*)

No! Elsa! Forgive! (*He sinks into drugged sleep again.*)

STILLWELL

You see. He keeps insisting to himself—

FATHER BAIRD
(*Defensively*)

That's a horrible charge for you to make, Doctor. Why, any one can see the poor boy is crazed with fear and grief.

138

STILLWELL

(*A bit ashamed*)

Sorry. But there have been times when I've had the strongest sense of—well, as he said, Something— (*Then curtly, feeling this makes him appear silly*) Afraid I've allowed this case to get on my nerves. Don't usually go in for psychic nonsense.

FATHER BAIRD

Your feeling isn't nonsense, Doctor.

STILLWELL

She won't forgive him. That's her trouble as well as his. (*He sighs, giving way for a moment to his own physical weariness*) A strange case. Too many undercurrents. The pneumonia has been more a means than a cause. (*With a trace of condescension*) More in your line. A little casting out of devils would have been of benefit—might still be.

FATHER BAIRD

Might still be. Yes.

STILLWELL

(*Exasperatedly*)

Damn it, I've seen many worse cases where the patient pulled through. If I could only get her will to live functioning again! If she'd forgive him and get that off her mind, I know she'd fight. (*He abruptly gets to his feet—curtly*) Well, talk won't help her, that's sure. I'll get back. (*He goes into the bedroom and closes the door silently behind him.* FATHER BAIRD *remains for a moment staring sadly at the floor. In the bedroom,* STILLWELL *goes to the bedside. The* NURSE *gets up and he speaks to her in a whisper, hears what she has to report, gives her some quick instructions. She goes to the bathroom. He sits in the chair by the bed and feels* ELSA's *pulse. The* NURSE *comes back and hands him a hypodermic needle. He administers this in* ELSA's *arm. She moans and her body twitches for a second. He sits, watching her face worriedly, his fingers on her wrist. In the study,* FATHER BAIRD *starts to pace back and forth, frowning, his face tense, feeling desperately that he is facing inevitable tragedy, that he must do something to thwart it at once. He stops at the foot of the chaise-longue and stares down at the sleeping* JOHN. *Then he prays*)

FATHER BAIRD

Dear Jesus, grant me the grace to bring Jack back to Thee. Make him see that Thou, alone, hast the words of Eternal Life, the power still to save—

LOVING
(*His eyes fixed on* JOHN's *face in the same stare—speaks as if in answer to* FATHER BAIRD's *prayer*)
Nothing can save her.

JOHN
(*Shuddering in his sleep*)

No!

LOVING
Her end in your story is coming true. It was a cunning method of murder!

FATHER BAIRD
(*Horrified*)

Jack!

JOHN

(*With a tortured cry that starts him awake*)
No! It's a lie! (*He stares around him at the air, as if he were trying to see some presence he feels there*) Liar! Murderer! (*Suddenly he seems to see* FATHER BAIRD *for the first time—with a cry of appeal—brokenly*) Uncle! For God's sake, help me! I—I feel I'm going mad!

FATHER BAIRD

(*Eagerly*)
If you would only let me help you, Jack! If you would only be honest with yourself and admit the truth in your own soul now, for Elsa's sake—while there is still time.

JOHN

(*Frightenedly*)
Still time? What do you mean? Is she—worse?

FATHER BAIRD

No. You've only been sleeping a few minutes. There has been no change.

JOHN

Then why did you say—?

FATHER BAIRD

Because I have decided you must be told the truth now the truth you already know in your heart.

JOHN

What—truth?

FATHER BAIRD

It is the crisis. Human science has done all it can to save her. Her life is in the hands of God now.

LOVING

There is no God!

FATHER BAIRD
(*Sternly*)

Do you dare say that—now!

JOHN
(*Frightenedly*)

No—I—I don't know what I'm saying— It isn't I —

FATHER BAIRD
(*Recovering himself—quietly*)

No. I know you couldn't blaspheme at such a time—not your true self.

LOVING
(*Angrily*)

It is my true self—my only self! And I see through your stupid trick—to use the fear of death to—

FATHER BAIRD

It's the hatred you once gave your soul to which speaks, not you! (*Pleadingly*) I implore you to cast that evil from your soul! If you would only pray!

LOVING
(*Fiercely*)

No!

142

DAYS WITHOUT END

JOHN

(*Stammers torturedly*)

I—I don't know— I can't think!

FATHER BAIRD

(*Intensely*)

Pray with me, Jack. (*He sinks to his knees*) Pray that Elsa's life may be spared to you! It is only God Who can open her heart to forgiveness and give her back the will to live! Pray for His forgiveness, and He will have compassion on you! Pray to Him Who is Love. Who is Infinite Tenderness and Pity!

JOHN

(*Half-slipping to his knees—longingly*)

Who is Love! If I could only believe again!

FATHER BAIRD

Pray for your lost faith and it will be given you!

LOVING

(*Sneeringly*)

You forget I once prayed to your God and His answer was hatred and death—and a mocking laughter!

JOHN

(*Starts up from his half-kneeling position, under the influence of this memory*)

Yes, I prayed then. No. It's no good, Uncle. I can't believe. (*Then suddenly—with eagerness*) Let Him prove to me His Love exists! Then I will believe in Him again!

143

FATHER BAIRD

You may not bargain with your God, Jack. (*He gets wearily to his feet, his shoulders bowed, looking tragically old and beaten—then with a last appeal*) But I beseech you still! I warn you!—before it's too late!—look into your soul and force yourself to admit the truth you find there—the truth you have yourself revealed in your story where the man, who is you, goes to the church and, at the foot of the Cross is granted the grace of faith again!

LOVING

In a moment of stupid madness! But remember that is not the end!

FATHER BAIRD
(*Ignoring this*)

There is a fate in that story, Jack—the fate of the will of God made manifest to you through the secret longing of your own heart for faith! Take care! It has come true so far, and I am afraid if you persist in your mad denial of Him and your own soul, you will have willed for yourself the accursed end of that man—and for Elsa, death!

JOHN
(*Terrified*)

Stop! Stop talking damned nonsense! (*Distractedly*) Leave me alone! I'm sick of your damned croaking! You're lying! Stillwell said there was no danger! She's asleep! She's getting better! (*Then terrified again*) What made you say, a fate in my story—the will of God? Good God, that's—that's nonsense! I— (*He starts for the bedroom door*) I'm going back to her. There's Something—

FATHER BAIRD
(*Tries to hold him back*)
You can't go there now, Jack.

JOHN
(*Pushing him roughly away*)
Leave me alone! (*He opens the bedroom door and lurches in. LOVING has come around behind the table and slips in after him. FATHER BAIRD, recovering from the push which has sent him back against the table, front, comes quickly to the doorway.*)
(*As JOHN comes in, STILLWELL turns from where he sits beside the bedside, a look of intense anger and exasperation on his face. JOHN, as soon as he enters, falls under the atmosphere of the sick-room, his wildness drops from him and he looks at STILLWELL with pleading eyes.*)

STILLWELL
(*Giving up getting him out again as hopeless, makes a gesture for him to be silent*)
Ssshh! (*The NURSE looks at JOHN with shocked rebuke. STILLWELL motions JOHN to sit down. He does so meekly, sinking into the chair at right, center. LOVING stands behind the chair. FATHER BAIRD, after a look into the room to see if his help is needed, exchanges a helpless glance with STILLWELL, and then, turning back into the study but leaving the communicating door ajar, goes back as far as the table. There, after a mo-*

145

*ment's pause, he bows his head and begins praying silently to
himself. In the bedroom,* STILLWELL *turns back to his patient.
There is a pause of silent immobility in the room.* JOHN's *eyes
are fixed on* ELSA's *face with a growing terror.* LOVING *stares
over his head with cold, still eyes.*)

JOHN

(*In a low, tense voice—as if he were thinking aloud*)
A fate in my story—the will of God! Something— (*He
shudders.*)

LOVING

(*In the same low tone, but with a cold, driving intensity*)
She will soon be dead.

JOHN

No!

LOVING

What will you do then? Love will be lost to you forever.
You will be alone again. There will remain only the anguish
of endless memories, endless regrets—a torturing remorse for
murdered happiness!

JOHN

I know! For God's sake, don't make me think—

LOVING

(*Coldly remorseless—sneeringly*)
Do you think you can choose your stupid end in your story
now, when you have to live it?—on to Hercules? But if you
love her, how can you desire to go on—with all that was Elsa
rotting in her grave behind you!

146

JOHN

(*Torturedly*)

No! I can't! I'll kill myself!

ELSA

(*Suddenly moans frightenedly*)

No, John! No!

LOVING

(*Triumphantly*)

Ah! At last you accept the true end! At last you see the empty posing of your old ideal about man's duty to go on for Life's sake, your meaningless gesture of braving fate—a childish nose-thumbing at Nothingness at which Something laughs with a weary scorn! (*He gives a low, scornful laugh*) Shorn of your boastful words, all it means is to go on like an animal in dumb obedience to the law of the blind stupidity of life that it must live at all costs! But where will you go—except to death? And why should you wait for an end you know when it is in your power to grasp that end—now!

ELSA

(*Again moans frightenedly*)

No, John—no!—please, John!

LOVING

Surely you cannot be afraid of death. Death is not the dying. Dying is life, its last revenge upon itself. But death is what the dead know, the warm, dark womb of Nothingness—the Dream in which you and Elsa may sleep as one forever, beyond fear of separation!

147

JOHN

(Longingly)

Elsa and I—forever beyond fear!

LOVING

Dust within dust to sleep!

JOHN

(Mechanically)

Dust within dust. (*Then frightenedly questioning*) Dust? (*A shudder runs over him and he starts as if awakening from sleep*) Fool! Can the dust love the dust? No! (*Desperately*) O God, have pity! Show me the way!

LOVING

(Furiously—as if he felt himself temporarily beaten)

Coward!

JOHN

If I could only pray! If I could only believe again!

LOVING

You cannot!

JOHN

A fate in my story, Uncle said—the will of God!—I went to the church—a fate in the church— (*He suddenly gets to his feet as if impelled by some force outside him. He stares before him with obsessed eyes*) Where I used to believe, where I used to pray!

LOVING

You insane fool! I tell you that's ended!

148

JOHN

If I could see the Cross again—

LOVING

(*With a shudder*)

No! I don't want to see! I remember too well!—when Father and Mother—!

JOHN

Why are you so afraid of Him, if—

LOVING

(*Shaken—then with fierce defiance*)

Afraid? I who once cursed Him, who would again if— (*Then hurriedly catching himself*) But what superstitious nonsense you make me remember. He doesn't exist!

JOHN

(*Takes a step toward the door*)

I am going!

LOVING

(*Tries to bar his path*)

No!

JOHN

(*Without touching him, makes a motion of pushing him aside*)

I am going. (*He goes through the door to the study, moving like one in a trance, his eyes fixed straight before him.* LOVING *continues to try to bar his path, always without touching him.* FATHER BAIRD *looks up as they pass the table.*)

LOVING

(*In impotent rage*)

No! You coward!

(JOHN *goes out the door in rear of study and* LOVING *is forced out before him.*)

FATHER BAIRD

(*Starting after him*)

Jack! (*But he turns back in alarm as, in the bedroom,* ELSA *suddenly comes out of the half-coma she is in with a cry of terror and, in spite of* STILLWELL, *springs up to a half-sitting position in bed, her staring eyes on the doorway to the study.*)

ELSA

John! (*Then to* STILLWELL) Oh, please! Look after him! He might— John! Come back! I'll forgive!

STILLWELL

(*Soothingly*)

There, don't be frightened. He's only gone to lie down for a while. He's very tired. (FATHER BAIRD *has come in from the study and is approaching the bed.* STILLWELL, *with a significant look, calls on him for confirmation*) Isn't that right, Father?

FATHER BAIRD

Yes, Elsa.

ELSA

(*Relieved*)

Oh. (*She smiles faintly*) Poor John. I'm so sorry. Tell him he mustn't worry. I understand now. I love—I forgive. (*She sinks back and closes her eyes.* STILLWELL *reaches for her wrist in alarm, but as he feels her pulse his expression changes to one of excited surprise.*)

FATHER BAIRD

(*Misreading his look—in a frightened whisper*)
Merciful God! She isn't—?

STILLWELL

No. She's asleep. (*Then with suppressed excitement*) That's done it! She'll want to live now!

FATHER BAIRD

God be praised! (STILLWELL, *his air curtly professional again turns and whispers some orders to the* NURSE.)

Curtain

ACT FOUR

Scene II

Scene—*A section of the interior of an old church. A side wall runs diagonally back from left, front, two-thirds of the width of the stage, where it meets an end wall that extends back from right, front. The walls are old gray stone. In the middle of the side wall is a great cross, its base about five feet from the floor, with a life-size figure of Christ, an exceptionally fine piece of wood carving. In the middle of the end wall is an arched doorway. On either side of this door, but high up in the wall, their bases above the level of the top of the doorway, are two narrow, stained-glass windows.*

It is a few minutes after the close of the preceding scene. The church is dim and empty and still. The only light is the reflection of the dawn, which, stained by the color in the windows, falls on the wall on and around the Cross.

The outer doors beyond the arched doorway are suddenly pushed open with a crash and JOHN *and* LOVING *appear in the doorway.* LOVING *comes first, retreating backward before* JOHN *whom he desperately, but always without touching him, endeavors to keep from entering the church. But* JOHN *is the stronger now and, the same look of obsessed resolution in his eyes, he forces* LOVING *back.*

LOVING

(*As they enter—desperately, as if he were becoming exhausted by the struggle*)

You fool! There is nothing here but hatred!

JOHN

No! There was love! (*His eyes fasten themselves on the Cross and he gives a cry of hope*) The Cross!

LOVING

The symbol of hate and derision!

JOHN

No! Of love! (LOVING *is forced back until the back of his head is against the foot of the Cross.* JOHN *throws himself on his knees before it and raises his hands up to the figure of Christ in supplication*) Mercy! Forgive!

LOVING

(*Raging*)

Fool! Grovel on your knees! It is useless! To pray, one must believe!

JOHN

I have come back to Thee!

LOVING

Words! There is nothing!

JOHN

Let me believe in Thy love again!

LOVING

You cannot believe!

JOHN

(Imploringly)

O God of Love, hear my prayer!

LOVING

There is no God! There is only death!

JOHN

(More weakly now)

Have pity on me! Let Elsa live!

LOVING

There is no pity! There is only scorn!

JOHN

Hear me while there is still time! *(He waits, staring at the Cross with anguished eyes, his arms outstretched. There is a pause of silence.)*

LOVING

(With triumphant mockery)

Silence! But behind it I hear mocking laughter!

JOHN

(Agonized)

No! *(He gives way, his head bowed, and sobs heartbrokenly —then stops suddenly, and looking up at the Cross again, speaks sobbingly in a strange humble tone of broken reproach)* O Son of Man, I am Thou and Thou art I! Why hast Thou forsaken me? O Brother Who lived and loved and suffered and died with us, Who knoweth the tortured hearts of men, canst Thou not forgive—now—when I surrender all to Thee— when I have forgiven Thee—the love that Thou once took from me!

154

LOVING

(*With a cry of hatred*)

No! Liar! I will never forgive!

JOHN

(*His eyes fixed on the face of the Crucified suddenly lighting up as if he now saw there the answer to his prayer—in a voice trembling with awakening hope and joy*)

Ah! Thou hast heard me at last! Thou hast not forsaken me! Thou hast always loved me! I am forgiven! I can forgive myself—through Thee! I can believe!

LOVING

(*Stumbles weakly from beneath the Cross*)

No! I deny! (*He turns to face the Cross with a last defiance*) I defy Thee! Thou canst not conquer me! I hate Thee! I curse Thee!

JOHN

No! I bless! I love!

LOVING

(*As if this were a mortal blow, seems to sag and collapse—with a choking cry*)

No!

JOHN

(*With a laugh that is half sob*)

Yes! I see now! At last I see! I have always loved! O Lord of Love, forgive Thy poor blind fool!

LOVING

No! (*His legs crumple under him, he slumps to his knees beside* JOHN, *as if some invisible force crushed him down.*)

JOHN

(*His voice rising exultantly, his eyes on the face of the Crucified*)

Thou art the Way—the Truth—the Resurrection and the Life, and he that believeth in Thy Love, his love shall never die!

LOVING

(*Faintly, at last surrendering, addressing the Cross not without a final touch of pride in his humility*)

Thou hast conquered, Lord. Thou art—the End. Forgive— the damned soul—of John Loving! (*He slumps forward to the floor and rolls over on his back, dead, his head beneath the foot of the Cross, his arms outflung so that his body forms another cross.* JOHN *rises from his knees and stands with arms stretched up and out, so that he, too, is like cross. While this is happening the light of the dawn on the stained-glass windows swiftly rises to a brilliant intensity of crimson and green and gold, as if the sun had risen. The gray walls of the church, particularly the wall where the Cross is, and the face of the Christ shine with this radiance.*)

(JOHN LOVING—*he, who had been only* JOHN—*remains standing with his arms stretched up to the Cross, an expression of mystic exaltation on his face. The corpse of* LOVING *lies at the foot of the Cross, like a cured cripple's testimonial offering in a shrine.*)

156

(FATHER BAIRD *comes in hurriedly through the arched doorway. He stops on seeing* JOHN LOVING, *then comes quietly up beside him and stares searchingly into his face. At what he sees there he bows his head and his lips move in grateful prayer.* JOHN LOVING *is oblivious to his presence.*)

FATHER BAIRD

(Finally taps him gently on the shoulder)

Jack.

JOHN LOVING

(Still in his ecstatic mystic vision—strangely)

I am John Loving.

FATHER BAIRD

(Stares at him—gently)

It's all right now, Jack. Elsa will live.

JOHN LOVING

(Exaltedly)

I know! Love lives forever! Death is dead! Ssshh! Listen!
Do you hear?

FATHER BAIRD

Hear what, Jack?

JOHN LOVING

Life laughs with God's love again! Life laughs with love!

Curtain